STAYING IN CHARGE

STAYING IN CHARGE

Practical Plans for the End of Your Life

KAREN ORLOFF KAPLAN, M.P.H., Sc.D

AND

CHRISTOPHER LUKAS

WILEY

John Wiley & Sons, Inc.

Published by John Wiley & Sons, Inc., Hoboken, New Jersey
Published simultaneously in Canada

The authors gratefully acknowledge the following for permission to quote from:

That You May Live Long: Caring for Our Aging Parents, Caring for Ourselves, edited by Richard F. Address and Hara E. Person. Used by permission of the Union of American Hebrew Congregations Press.

Covering the Issues of Death and Dying: A Journalist's Resource Guide, published, with support from The Robert Wood Johnson Foundation, by the Radio and Television News Directors Foundation, Washington, D.C., 1998.

Peaceful Dying by Daniel R. Tobin. Copyright © 1999 by Daniel R. Tobin. Reprinted by permission of Perseus Books Publishers, a member of Perseus Books, L.L.C.

"Being a Health Care Agent" and "Choosing a Health Care Agent" by the New York Citizen's Committee on Health Care Decisions.

"Crafting a Vessel for My Father" told by Peggy King-Jorde, "I Know How I Want to Die" told by Elena Lister, from *Giving a Voice to Sorrow* by Steve Zeitlin and Ilana Harlow, copyright © 2001 by Steve Zeitlin and Ilana Harlow. Used by permission of Perigee Books, an imprint of Penguin Putnam, Inc.

Giorgianni S., Grana J., et al. "A Profile of Caregiving in America." *The Pfizer Journal*. New York, NY: Pfizer Inc., 1997. Available at: www.thepfizerjournal.com

Design and production by Navta Associates, Inc.

For general information about our other products and services, please contact our Customer Care Department within the United States at (800) 762-2974, outside the United States at (317) 572-3993 or fax (317) 572-4002.

Wiley also publishes its books in a variety of electronic formats. Some content that appears in print may not be available in electronic books. For more information about Wiley products, visit our web site at www.wiley.com.

ISBN 978-1-63026-170-2

Printed in the United States of America

10 9 8 7 6 5 4 3 2 1

For our families

How does one live with illness that will likely end life, but not yet, and not at any knowable time? What happens when we realize that death may not be so far away as we thought it was? How do we ask and answer the most important question—"How do I want to live now?" The answer will be different for everyone but most people, once they've been posed the question, start thinking in a fresh way and start living with a new purpose. It's a nice lesson for all of us that one healthy response to facing a life-threatening illness is to live intensely and to live fully.

—Linda Emanuel, M.D.

The most important thing from an emotional point of view is not to be afraid to confront what this all means. We don't make wills because we're afraid of dying; and we don't make living wills because we don't want to discuss it, and our kids don't want us to talk to them about those things. But it's paramount. We have to have the courage to say, "I've got to think about this!"

—Anita, health care proxy for her mother

I think that what families, what patients, what all of us can do as individuals who will be facing the end of life some day is to take a step back. Think of death as a normal process of living, and think how we would like that journey toward death to be. I have seen people do it and it is amazing. They've done it under the worst circumstances and the most horrendous diseases. And they are able to do it because they've made a commitment to talking with their families, to talking with their providers and saying what it is they want and how they want it to be.

—Anna Moretti, R.N., A.N.P., J.D.

CONTENTS

INTRODUCTION

There may come a time when you are diagnosed with a serious illness. You realize that you are, after all, mortal. You realize that decisions have to be made about how to cure that illness, or how to face the likelihood that that illness will be with you for a long time, maybe the rest of your life.

And there may come a time when your illness is so severe that you know it is your final illness.

There may come a time when you can no longer make all health decisions for yourself.

There may come a time when *cure* fades as an option and *quality of life* becomes paramount.

There may come a time when you or others have to decide whether you go to a hospital, a hospice, or a nursing home.

And at any one of these times, you may realize you don't have all the information you need to make the next decision or cope with a crisis.

This book is designed to help you start thinking about these moments in the last years of your journey and to start talking about the things that are important to you. It's time to care—about your loved ones and about yourself.

It's time to think about what the words "quality of life" mean to you.

It's time to think about how to *live* with life-threatening illnesses, not just how to die with them.

At one time we considered calling this book *Dying 101: Getting It Right the First Time*, because in a way finding out about serious illness and how to make mortality less burdensome is as much a course of study as any other transition in life. And while, of course, death never can be conquered, the fears about it and the transition to it can be tempered by understanding.

But this book is about a lot more than dying—far more. It's about how to think about the future, how to take steps to avoid some of the things you fear most about being seriously ill. It's about learning how to gather forces around you so that you're supported by your loved ones. And it's about how to support others.

Learning about chronic illnesses and about what finally happens to all of us—the dying process—should not be a strange concept. After all, you take the time and opportunity to learn about all sorts of things: about pregnancy and birth, raising infants and adolescents; about how the planets work, who the founding fathers were, why "ain't" isn't grammatical. You go to high school, perhaps to college. You learn law and medicine and engineering, how to tie your shoes, dial the phone, use a computer. The most intricate details of your lives—from sex to menopause, from keeping a checkbook to filling out a tax form—*all* have to be learned.

Frankly, dying is too important a part of the life cycle to let it happen haphazardly, without planning, without thinking about it, without *learning* about it. Besides, "dying," as we see it, is about a long, long period of time. It's about your life from the moment you have a diagnosis of any potentially life-threatening illness, no matter what your age. It's about months and months, and years and years for most of us. "Dying" is a matter of emotional and spiritual approach, not simply a physical end to life.

So before you close this book and put it away (in fear or denial), let us tell you that this book isn't about the last breaths you will take. It's about learning to *live* with dying, about taking the time to think about how long you have to live, and—because of modern medicine—how much time may be spent dying. It's about thinking about the unmentionable so that you will not have to be afraid during your last twenty or thirty years of living. It's about preventing the things you most fear about dying:

- Being alone
- Losing control
- Being in pain
- Being without spiritual peace

This book will tell you why you can

- Be certain you have company when you are ill or dying
- Be almost entirely pain-free
- Avoid some anxiety and panic if you are diagnosed with a serious illness

Finally, it will tell you how to protect yourself and your loved ones from the conspiracy of silence that surrounds dying and death.

But there's more: we will also look at the spiritual and emotional reserves that you possess to deal with the approaching end of life. We will tell you about the corps of trained people waiting to make the last chapter of life easier for you.

Equally important, we will help you see that there is a great deal of *living* going on during the last years, months, days, even hours of that chapter. When you are faced with a serious illness, there is no reason to give up living a full life. That's more true than ever now, as modern medicine takes what used to be terminal illnesses and turns them into long-term, chronic illnesses, where people are more or less sick for years and years. You may have a disease that has symptoms that must be attended to, but you can stay alive and remarkably active for months and years to come. Even the most virulent and frightening of diseases—cancer and AIDS—have different timetables, depending on the type, when it is discovered, the state of medical science, and your response to a particular medication or series of medications or other treatments. In other words, while we write here about dying and death, in the chapters that follow we will talk mainly about how to go on living while you're dying, how to deal with the emotional and physical discomfort of disease while learning how to make life more enjoyable *right from the first day of diagnosis of a serious illness.*

We hope to relieve you of the need to stay in denying silence. We hope to help you learn to communicate with those you love and those who love you.

Dying and all that may lead up to it is a chapter of life about which much can and should be learned. This book is designed to open up this chapter so that you can be prepared, take control, and use your final years and months to create bonds with family and friends, examine the best parts of your life, and open yourself up for yet one more important experience.

We will lay out facts, describe minefields, and tell a few well-chosen, true-life stories about people who have shown the way; but here's an important note: This book is not about what other people have done to make serious illness or dying less painful or more spiritual. It is about what *you* need to know to make *your* last chapter of life more fruitful, less lonely, more productive, more integral to the rest of your years.

1

Why We Wrote This Book

W ho we are and the personal reasons why we wrote this book are germane. For one thing, men and women often approach questions of illness quite differently. For instance, many men tend to deny more than do women, or fear that talking about death will cause it to happen. Many women think in terms of a "good death," meaning comfort and peace and preparedness of spirit as well as body. Women often make end-of-life decisions more in terms of their children's and their spouses' needs than do men. Men often want to prolong life as much as possible, no matter the pain. Women take pain into consideration. And so on. Which is why we thought having both a man and a woman write this book would be very helpful.

One of us is a woman in her early sixties, a social worker whose professional work is day-to-day involvement with the legal, social, medical, ethical, and personal ramifications of end-of-life decisionmaking. As president of the not-for-profit organization Last Acts Partnership (advocating quality end-of-life care), she spends her days trying to improve care near the end of life for all Americans. She tries to get people to take control by thinking about issues they would rather hide in the deep recesses of their minds, and to alert society to the necessity of discourse about those matters.

The other author is a man in his late sixties whose work as a writer and as a television producer has taken him to scenes of serious illness and death, and who has previously written a book about death. Together we hope to be able to guide you through these labyrinths.

Karen's Story

Some years ago, just after I turned fifty, my mother went into the hospital with a serious illness. Because she was close to eighty and had been ill for some time, we were not surprised by her turn for the worse, nor would we have been astonished if she had died quickly. That was not the case, however. Because of modern medical care and my mother's indomitable spirit and constitution, she lingered, and as she lingered one body system after another gave out, first her kidneys, then her lungs, then her heart. At one point the doctors told me that my mother would have to be put on a respirator; otherwise, she would die immediately.

Up until that time, I had assumed her doctors would make such decisions, since they had been treating her for many years. But these physicians now expected me to tell them what I wanted them to do. I had never discussed such things with my mother. I didn't know whether—had she been conscious and able to speak for herself—she would have wanted to be kept alive so painfully with so little to gain, or would have wanted to be allowed to die peacefully. After much inner turmoil and effort to guess what Mother would have wanted, I asked the doctors to try a respirator and see what happened.

Aroused by the strange discomfort of having the respirator tubes inserted, my mother struggled, obviously in pain. When the tubes were removed to see if she could breathe on her own, she told us in no uncertain terms that we should *never* attach her to any machines again. Despite all loving intentions, I had guessed incorrectly. And so we followed her wishes; disconnected the tubes, the electrodes, and needles; and gave her enough morphine to keep her totally comfortable. That's how my mother died, at last, peacefully.

While I sat in the hospital waiting room and tried to decide what I should do, I listened to others whose loved ones were in intensive care. Most of those waiting were women—daughters, sisters, aunts, mothers, lovers—and I became aware that they, too, did not know what to do, had not thought about such end-of-life decisionmaking, and had not discussed such issues with those loved ones who were now unable to say what they wanted.

Often the physicians were of little help, mainly because they saw their job as maintaining life, even when all that was being extended was the dying process. The relatives and loved ones were those who had to decide, and they had little to go on.

It seems fitting, then, that I now find myself president of an organization whose purpose is to help people of all ages think about these issues in advance, so that their loved ones and the hospitals and hospices they eventually turn to can know what to do to help them live the last chapter of their lives comfortably and peacefully. We exist to help everyone exercise his or her right to participate fully in decisions about their medical treatment at the end of life, to secure adequate pain medication and other appropriate comfort care, and to be treated with dignity and respect.

Christopher's Story

In 1992, I was diagnosed with non-Hodgkin's lymphoma. I was fifty-seven.

Non-Hodgkin's lymphoma is actually fifteen different kinds of cancer that can be very virulent and fast, or slow and not too dangerous, but even the least potent has to be caught and treated. While the doctors at Memorial Sloan Kettering were trying to decide exactly what to do with my version, which was slow-growing and discovered early on, I was trying to decide how to come to terms with death.

It had never occurred to me that I might get a serious ailment before I was in my eighties. I have one of those natural builds that makes heart problems a negligible possibility, none of my immediate family had died from cancer, and I wasn't overweight or underweight or suffering from anemia or any other obvious physical problem. In other words, like many, I thought I would either fall off a cliff on a trip somewhere or die in my sleep of "old age."

Think again. Here I was in "middle age" being told that I had a chronic cancer that could not be cured. It could be held back, retarded, dismissed from my body for a while, but most likely it would return.

So my first thought was that I was, after all, mortal. My second thought was that I was going to die—soon. My third thought was, "Why, me?"

I slept poorly, worried about what to tell my wife and daughters about my chances of survival, and got swept off my feet emotionally.

These were the reactions that many if not most people diagnosed with a serious disease find themselves facing: anxiety, depression, anger, panic over loss of control. I was forced to reevaluate myself and the way I had led my life, and to ponder my position in the universe. The news was so dispiriting that I found myself too depressed to do daily tasks, to communicate with my family and friends, to attend to business.

At the time I was diagnosed, I didn't know about advance directives—living wills and medical powers of attorney. I didn't know how to think about pain. And I certainly had never thought about cutting back at work or making plans for emotional or spiritual help in the face of such a dreaded disease.

What I learned in the months to follow was that it doesn't really matter how serious or hopeful the diagnosis; the first time you are told that *you* have cancer is a devastating experience. You can't hear that you're probably not going to die from this disease. You can't hear the encouraging words from friends, family, and doctors. All you want is to be *cured*!

Slowly, I began to realize that I wasn't going to die. I began to believe that my doctors were going to save me; that my family was telling me they loved me; that I could relax a little and enjoy what was left of my life.

I decided in that year of recognizing mortality that I would be as prepared as I could be for the time when death did come knocking at the door with more serious intentions. I would write a living will, appoint someone to stand in for me if I couldn't speak or think for myself, get long-term health insurance so that I could be taken care of at home should I get more seriously ill, and make my relationships with loved ones as close as I could.

When Karen Kaplan asked me to write this book with her, I quickly agreed. I am aware that thinking about death is very difficult for many men. We fear that if we talk about death, it will come sooner, or make us more afraid of the end. In fact, the opposite is true: talking about dying and death can be reassuring. And thinking and planning for it well in advance can be more than reassuring: it can save lots of pain and anxiety. It can save loved ones lots of regret, and can improve our lives and others'.

This book is a way to share some of what I learned when I became ill, of how to think about dying and death—of how to live a life as fully as possible while knowing that another disease or threat of death could be around the corner, how to gather friends and family and health care workers around the campfire to guide and protect.

Luckily, I was merely tapped on the shoulder, given a warning, and awakened to the need to think ahead, to plan ahead, to make myself as educated as I can be about the events at the end of the journey.

The lymphoma of 1992 wasn't the end of it. Eight years later, I found out I had prostate cancer. Forty days of radiation seems to have sent that into deep remission.

But even that wasn't the end of it: As we were revising this book for publication, in the winter of 2003, a routine examination showed some suspicious nodes and lesions in my interior. After many tests, the result was that I had to have a painful abdominal operation to remove some of the threatening material. After six days in the hospital, I returned to work, more knowledgeable than ever that:

- Chronic illness is by no means the same as a death sentence. It is not equivalent to dying. In 1992, despite a cancer diagnosis, I had many years to go. I still do.
- Pain and loneliness can be frightening, but there are ways to greatly alleviate the symptoms and the fears.
- Learning to ask the right questions and demand the right answers is a big part of banishing the fears we talk about in the next chapter.

2

OBSTACLES TO GOOD CARE

In 2003, Last Acts Partnership, a national coalition striving to make care and caring near the end of life better for all of us, discovered through a state-by-state review that a significant number of Americans, including those who had recently lost a loved one, are dissatisfied with the way the country's health care system provides care to the dying.

Each state received letter grades on each of eight key elements of end-of-life care.

Overall findings? At best, end-of-life care in the United States is mediocre. Specifically:

- Some states create bureaucratic hurdles that make it difficult for patients to express their preferences or to designate surrogate decisionmakers.
- Although most Americans would prefer to be at home with loved ones in their final days, only about 25 percent of Americans will die at home.
- Hospice programs, considered the "gold standard" for end-of-life care, are not widely used. Worse, the average length of stay under a hospice program is well below the sixty days considered necessary for people to get maximum benefit.
- Nationwide, too many people are treated in intensive care units (ICUs) in their last six months of life. This is often at the expense of attention to quality of life, and is not what patients have said they want.

- Nearly half of the 1.6 million Americans living in nursing homes have persistent pain that is not adequately treated.
- Six in ten Americans give our overall end-of-life health care system a rating of only fair or lower.

This report made apparent what you may have already known: if you ask friends and neighbors why they aren't getting good health care, the answer is almost always "The system."

With regard to end-of-life care, we want to look in this chapter at where the system is broken, where it's being mended, and where other, equally important obstacles to dealing well with chronic and terminal illnesses come into play.

When the System Gets in the Way

Advances in medical treatment—new technologies—are often thought of as the medical system's primary stumbling block. It's the system's Achilles' heel: our vaunted ability to keep you alive on tubes or with cutting-edge care *just because it's possible.*

Medical schools *teach* technology. Medical students *learn* that technology. The profession *practices* technology. It's built into the medical system. It enables us to have hip replacements, artificial hearts, and much more.

But technology can lead to *too much treatment*—treatment that takes people into the intensive care unit during the last days of life, stretching out their time on earth, but not the *quality* of that time, and robbing them of the chance to say good-bye to loved ones.

Even some of the technological know-how given to people with chronic (i.e., long-term) illnesses is so intrusive and intense that it robs them of quality of life.

Much as this is talked about, and much as "the system" is moving to change the enormous emphasis on technology, it is a very proud element of America's medical prowess, which means that many within American medicine are not prepared to accept new ideas about these matters.

In short, technology's ability to keep people living longer and longer and to heal the seriously ill is profoundly wonderful, but you may not get to live your life as *you* choose. You may end up on support mechanisms in the ICU when you would prefer to be at home under hospice care, free of pain, but with those who are closest to you. You may not *want* another operation just because it's available. You may want to make a different set of choices right up until the end. There are other ways the medical system can work against your achieving quality of life at the end of life, including the way health care professionals are trained, communication within the system, and the values and attitudes of those who work inside it, as well as how the whole system is financed. Let's take a brief look at each.

Training

In 1998 only 4 out of 126 American medical schools required students to take even one course on care of the dying. Most textbooks didn't discuss it. Nurses also received precious little training in such matters. Today, programs like EPEC (Educating Physicians about End of Life Care) and ELNEC (End of Life Nursing Education Consortium) have begun rectifying this for those who have already left the training ground, while nursing schools and medical schools are beginning to make such courses mandatory. But a lot of physicians and nurses today are still in the dark about end-of-life care.

The Result: Care leading up to the end of your life may not incorporate all the new and creative ways that medicine now can handle the emotional, physical, and spiritual problems with which this book is concerned.

Communication with Your Primary Care Physician and Your Specialists

It's a common observation that we're long past the time of the friendly family doctor who knew all of your problems and your family's medical history to boot.

But you should still expect to be able to communicate with your doctor, to have him or her listen to and *hear* what you're saying. And vice versa, too. Yet you must have found that doesn't always happen: you don't always get the kind of listening that you want from your physicians, and perhaps, too, you don't speak up when you should.

The Result: When it comes to serious illness, communication can become more difficult than usual, and this can seriously hurt your chances of getting the best care. You and your physicians may talk at cross-purposes. You may not have a doctor who wants to hear about how much pain you are having, or about your fears.

How did this come about? For decades, medical schools did not teach how to communicate with a patient about the fact that he or she is dying. In fact, one of the greatest challenges has been to convince physicians that dying and death are not medical failures. Rather, they are part of life and should be treated as such. Physicians need to learn how to address them, not ignore them or flee from them.

Now, as Jamie Van Roenn, M.D., of the Robert H. Lurie Cancer Treatment Center at Northwestern University describes, some medical schools address this issue in their curriculum.

> In our medical school, I'm one of the teachers of a communication skills course. What we're doing is teaching students how to talk to patients, not specific medical things, but how you *communicate*. I tell them, you just go in there and be a human being. You listen and you ask. And when you ask, you stop and *listen* to the answer. If you don't listen you don't know anything.

Gwendolyn London, interim director of the Duke University Institute on Care at the End of Life, urges health care workers to break the glass wall between patient and professional.

> Get down off that pedestal. Take a seat so that you're on the same level as the patient. In addition to coming down to the person's level, physically, I think there is a very profound emotional and psychological piece: It's the idea of trying to connect with the person, one on one, coming to *where they are,* emotionally, as well as physically.

Values

There are many kinds of values that can get in the way of good treatment. Cultural values are one.

The Result: If you're a person of color or come from a culture where death is treated differently than in mainstream America, you may find that a physician doesn't understand your needs or treats you in a manner that is offensive or, at the least, not helpful. African Americans and Hispanics often find that doctors who don't listen carefully to *their* needs do not give them the kind of care they want. In another part of this book, we talk about how pain medication is often not administered equally across the population because of cultural misperceptions.

There are other values that can get in the way of good treatment.

Patients often report that physicians pay scant attention to *emotional* matters, such as worries about side effects of medicines, or depression and anxiety. To the doctor, these may be usual adjuncts to what they do every day. To you, however, they may be devastating. Having no sex drive, or having no zest for life, or being anxious all the time, can interfere with relationships with family members precisely at the time when their support is needed.

If communication is not free and clear between patients and doctors, these matters don't get addressed. Patients don't have vital information. Good choices cannot be made. Problems don't get solved.

Attitudes

Nurses, social workers, nurse's aides, and physicians go into the world of medicine wholeheartedly, with the best of intentions, but the system changes many of their personal views and submerges them beneath an institutional ethic focused on prolonging life, regardless of the futility or accompanying suffering, and no matter what any single patient might wish.

In the old days of "family doctors," we made the assumption that the physician knew best, and so we waited for him to tell us what we needed to know and, often, to make decisions for us. In more recent days, as we face the managed care dilemma of less time and less personal connection with our doctors, more and more responsibility has fallen to the patient. In fact, "patient autonomy" has become the mantra of the profession. To some extent, this has been welcomed by advocates for consumer power in medicine. But for others, it has been a way for doctors to avoid responsibility.

The Result: A mixed bag, depending on who the patient is and who the doctor is. Some doctors don't give enough information to the patient, but expect patients to make important decisions; others give too much and overburden the patients.

If the physician truly believes in patient autonomy, then he or she will be open and forthcoming about alternative treatment plans, and will discuss these plans and these options with the patient.

Too often, tales are told about doctors making decisions about a patient's care and treatment plan without consulting with the seriously ill patient, or ignoring the wishes of family members. While some of these stories are overblown, there are enough cases where the approach of a physician or nurse—whether because of training or religious or cultural upbringing—gets in the way of what a patient or a patient's family *wants.*

And unless family members and health care surrogates know exactly what they're doing and keep up the pressure, many loved ones will not get what they want.

Money

The system problems aren't only what doctors and nurses and hospitals do or don't do. It's also how we get good end-of-life care *paid for.*

Or, more likely, *don't,* for the fact is that millions of us are not insured, or are underinsured. And even with the best of insurance—private insurance for those who can afford it, Medicare for those over sixty-five—there are enormous problems getting paid when we need it, and for what we need.

Sometimes this is the fault of the wrangling going on in Congress over healthcare budgets; sometimes it's the fault of bureaucracy. Sometimes it's just local bookkeeping gone awry.

Take, for instance, the matter of long-term care insurance, which provides for your care at home or in a nursing facility and keeps you or your family from running through savings when you're seriously ill. Unless you purchase your own separate long-term-care insurance, long-term care is simply not covered. And most Americans don't have such insurance. We bet that *you* don't. It's very expensive when you're older—when you first think about it—so you may not be able to afford it. (Of course, when you're young and not thinking about these matters, it's very *inexpensive.*)

The Result: Half of all American families find that their savings are depleted when long-term illnesses occur.

The Patient's Own Obstacles to Good Care

Now it's time to discuss obstacles to good end-of-life care *outside* the system. For, whatever is wrong with our overall healthcare system, especially with end-of-life care, there are many barriers that stem from what *you* do or do not do; what *you* know or do not know. Only by being aware of these, and by making an effort to take charge of your own life and to fight to have your needs met during chronic or terminal illness, can you push aside some of the barriers that rest within the system.

Denial

When you are struck by a serious illness or accident that could lead to your death, denial is often an enemy of getting the kind of care you deserve. This is the almost automatic thinking your brain goes through when you are threatened with illness: "It's nothing. It'll go away." This kind of thinking isn't unique to any particular age group. It could happen when you're older, or younger. It could be a cancer, it could be Lou Gehrig's disease, it could be an ailment of the heart or lungs or intestinal system, or simply a bad accident. One day you believe you're healthy, the next day you find out that you're not.

The unwillingness to accept that you've got a medical problem is common. It's an understandable emotion, and comes from the terrible thought that lurks beneath—that we are mortal and will die sooner than we want to.

The Result: Denial is definitely a two-edged sword. A certain amount can be helpful. It can give you some protection against panic. It can allow you to figure out what to do and how to do it, and how much time you have to do it. The "I'm not dying" feeling may allow you to enter a state of mind that permits you to keep your cool and go about the business of planning what you would do *if* you were seriously ill.

On the other hand, wishing it weren't so keeps you and your family from believing that a serious physical illness has befallen you. This may prevent you from getting the help you need, or even from going to get a checkup at all. If you are clearheaded about this but your family isn't, your comfort level isn't helped by loved ones who deny that you're seriously ill or in pain, or insist that your physician has the wrong diagnosis. (Getting a second opinion is always a good idea, but running around looking for someone to give you good news may just be postponing the day you need to take stock of where you actually are.)

Emotional Shock Waves

When denial passes, serious emotional shock waves often occur. You now realize with no doubt that you are going to die someday, perhaps soon, and this acknowledgment can bring on huge amounts of anxiety, anger, or depression. Since this preview of death usually comes without warning and takes you by surprise, it can sweep you off your feet emotionally.

The Result: Very often these emotions can render you peculiarly unable to think clearly. A decision you could have made yesterday with only a moment's hesitation is now a huge dilemma. Just when you most need your intelligence, wit, and thinking power, you are robbed of them.

And if you haven't made plans for such eventualities, your emotional roller coaster will be all the more distressing. You will suddenly find that you have decisions to make for which your emotional state renders you remarkably unprepared. Which brings us to—

Lack of Planning, Lack of Knowledge

Perhaps, like most Americans, you have given very little thought to what you really want to have happen when you are dying:

- Where you wish to live during the final chapter of life
- Whom you want to be with you
- What resources you will use
- What you want done—or *not* done—to treat you

You just never wanted to *think* about dying and death. Not for yourself, not for your family. Your children, even if grown, don't want to contemplate what might happen when you get seriously ill. And you as parents certainly don't want to think about your children's deaths.

Goals are important. You *need* to think about dying and death, to take an internal inventory of your ideas about what values you want to preserve, what kind of care you do or do not want if you should be hit with a serious disease or have a debilitating and life-threatening accident. When the event occurs, as we suggested above, your emotional shock will interfere with your ability to get information and to make plans; lack of preparation for these eventualities, and unfamiliarity with the system, creates yet another obstacle.

Dr. Linda Emanuel, who runs Educating Physicians about End of Life Care (EPEC), thinks that many patients don't receive the kind of care they want and deserve because neither they nor their physicians have thought carefully about those goals. "Nothing makes sense," she says, "until you've got the goals right."

Clearly, denial and fear can keep you from planning ahead, from seeking advice and devising strategies that will help you in the years ahead.

The Result: *Unless you think ahead,* your desire to "die peacefully, at home" or even to "fight to the very end" will not happen. Despite changes currently ongoing in "the system," you won't get to choose either the peaceful sleep or the valiant fight.

Your Goal for Now

Many, many years ago—so they say—a man was traveling through the Arkansas countryside when a downpour began. He stopped at a friendly farmer's house for supper and noticed a large leak in the roof that dripped into several pots in the kitchen. When he asked why the farmer didn't fix the leak, the man looked at him with scorn: "You can't fix a roof when it's raining," he said. "Why not fix it when it's *not* raining?" the traveler asked. Again, a look of scorn. "Why, fellow, when it's not raining I don't need to fix it; it ain't leaking then."

So, in a similar way, you figure that when you're well, you don't need to think about being ill. And when you're ill you're too sick to do anything about it.

But it is possible to think ahead about these matters and actually do something about them before it rains. In order to make decisions, to have goals, you have to know the facts. And despite most Americans' desire to have a "good death," most don't have the knowledge they need.

For now, your goal is to be willing to read on—to be open to thinking about these matters. Ideally you'll begin to think about these matters while the sun still shines, when you're not under terrible emotional pressure, but if not, take advantage of medical turning points, such as those listed below, to think about the issues we raise in this book.

Turning Points

- *Serious symptoms*—when you or a physician notice something different in the way your body is behaving.
- *Diagnosis*—when tests determine exactly what is wrong with you.
- *Prognosis*—you're given an idea of what to do to treat your illness and how long you may have to deal with it. You are told that it's a chronic (lifelong) illness or an acute (life-threatening) one.
- *Treatment*—the period during which you and your health care team are

making an attempt to cure your illness. For a chronic illness, this could be years and years. For an advanced terminal illness, it could be only a few weeks or months.

- *Remission*—when your illness has stopped progressing for a long or short period.
- *Recurrence*—when your illness needs treatment again.
- *End of curative treatment*—either when your illness needs no further treatment or your illness is no longer treatable. This may signal immediate death, but it can equally be a period of some length, during which you will want to have other kinds of treatment, called "palliative care," treatments to which this book pays a great deal of attention.

3

THINKING AND TALKING ABOUT MORTALITY

The American population is aging. More and more of us are older than sixty-five. More and more of us are living into our nineties. That's good news, because it means that we're not dying as early as previous generations; we're healthier longer. And what's more, research demonstrates that growing older does not necessarily mean growing sicker or less vital.

That's right. Serious disease is not *increasing* in older people; it's declining. Or, rather, it's occurring at a later age than in previous generations, as our ability to prevent or treat illnesses improves.

The bad news is that you're mortal: no matter how much healthy food you eat, no matter how many vitamins you take, no matter how much good medical technology exists, someday you will die. The other bad news is that although you live longer and don't die until you're much older, you may get an illness which, in previous generations, would have killed you right away; now it may be chronic, long-lasting, and debilitating, causing great distress. In fact, most people these days do not die from acute illnesses. They die from chronic ones, illnesses that have gone on for a long time.

If, like most Americans, you have been most afraid of cancer, you need to be aware that people who die from cancer generally are able to carry on common activities up to two to three months before their death. People with chronic diseases, on the other hand, mostly are not able to do that. "People with heart disease or COPD go through periods of slowly declining health marked by sudden severe episodes of illness requiring hospitalization, from which the patient recovers. This pattern may repeat itself over and over, with the patient's overall health steadily declining, until the patient dies. For these individuals there is considerable uncertainty about when death is likely to occur," says the Department of Health and Human Services (HHS) in a recent report.

Why This Matters

An aging society, even one in the most technologically competent society in the world, is a mixed blessing.

The significance for you is that *not* planning ahead, *not* thinking or talking about what serious illnesses may bring and what you want when they come, will inhibit the kind of care you get and the quality of life you may have over years and years of living. Your fear of death may hinder you from getting good care.

If you're like most other Americans, you will have developed a strong antipathy to feelings of mortality. You run gingerly across the fallen log over the stream, duck when a tree limb falls, brake carefully on the road next to the cliff, wear protective gear in the factory, and train so that you, not the enemy, will survive the fierce battles of life. So agile are you at escaping death over your increasingly long life that you don't even talk about it or, in some cases, even think about it.

While decreasing the consciousness of death may appear to make your life easier, it actually makes you less likely to handle serious illness well; it can make dying more painful, more lonely, more out of control.

But *thinking* about death is not the same as death itself. And while you may be afraid of dying, you should not be afraid of *preparing* for dying. Despite superstitions to the contrary, you won't die simply because you want to prepare for bad times, any more than you'll die if you take out life insurance. In other words, silence is not golden, ignorance is not bliss.

Pretending that you are immortal isn't helpful. In fact, it's dangerous. The same HHS study we referred to above has lots of bad news about that:

- Fewer than half of severely or terminally ill patients studied have put on paper what kind of care they want or do not want when they're dying.

- Only 12 percent of patients who had put wishes on paper had received input from their physician.
- Health care providers and those speaking for patients unable to speak for themselves had difficulty knowing when to stop treatment and often waited until the patient was actively dying because they didn't know enough about a patient's wishes.

And, there are benefits of thinking ahead. Again, the HHS studies showed that discussing wishes ahead of time with doctors increased patient satisfaction among patients age 65 years and over. Patients who talked with their families or physicians about their preferences for end-of-life care and put those thoughts on paper:

- Had less fear and anxiety
- Felt they had more ability to influence and direct their medical care
- Believed that their physicians had a better understanding of their wishes
- Indicated a greater understanding and comfort level than they had before the discussion
- Conveyed to their loved ones a greater confidence to predict preferences and a stronger belief in the importance of having discussed wishes in advance
- Continued to discuss and talk about these concerns with their families.

"Such discussions enabled patients and families to reconcile their differences about end-of-life care and helped the family and physician come to agreement about what to do if they should need to make decisions for the patient," says the Department of Health and Human Services.

The Foreign Travel Analogy

Look at it in another way: when you take a vacation, heading off to France or Africa or Canada (or New York City), you are aware that different lands have different rules. Driving, insurance, currency, the legal status of women and children, the language—all may be quite strange, even startling. That's part of the fun of traveling. Still, if you go to many of these foreign lands without any groundwork, you might run into trouble for lack of preparation. You might get into embarrassing scrapes, sometimes into real trouble.

So you prepare by reading a guidebook, learning a smattering of the language, familiarizing yourself with the basic rules of the road.

When you are ill, you also journey to a world that is foreign, a land in which physicians and nurses use a special language that you cannot always decode. It is a culture all its own. It's doubly hard these days, when chronic illnesses can make it appear like you're dying one day and recovering the next. Dr. Joanne Lynn, a specialist in end-of-life care, tells us that "Only twenty percent of us die with a phase that is clearly 'dying.'" Heart, lung, and kidney diseases are not predictable, even by the most skilled physicians, who, Dr. Lynn says, miss the mark by a wide margin. "Make peace with God and be ready to go, but also ready to stay," she says in a dry statement of conclusion to a major report on end-of-life care.

Quality of Life

Just what is it that you want when you do think ahead? Are you like the 71 percent of Americans who, in a survey in *Modern Maturity* magazine, said that there was a point at which costly health treatments should end, and that at that point they wanted powerful painkillers to be used? Or those who said they were afraid of "lingering" and "being kept alive" after they could no longer enjoy their lives? This desire for quality of life above a longer life *without* quality has become more prevalent over the past decade as more and more people become aware of the dying process, and of ways to improve living during that process.

> Quality of life means making the time that patients have remaining in their life meaningful. It has to be defined in coordination with the stage we are at in our life. Our physical strength and health may not be as important as relationships, as attending to the needs of our family, as other things.
>
> —Michael Preodor, M.D., President, Horizon Hospice

It became really clear that for my wife, what defined quality was the ability to interact meaningfully with other people. Not just to sort of smile and blink her eyes you know, lie there, waiting to die. But to enjoy, to take pleasure, to get a hug from a grandchild. To come home and talk quietly with me. To visit with friends. As long as possible, to work. That was real meaning to her.

—Husband of a patient with cancer

- The people in the *Modern Maturity* survey also said that communication was of "overwhelming importance." They wanted their loved ones to be "participants" in the dying process, and that included lots of talking back and forth.
- Pain was also a main concern, as were breathlessness, diarrhea, and vomiting.
- Participants wanted to retain control of end-of-life decisions as long as possible, and then have their health care agent do so.
- And, as might be expected, patients were concerned about the financial and emotional burdens their dying would cause to their family members.

The survey specifically dealt with the time when cure is no longer feasible or likely. But, as we have said, for most of us there are many years prior to that situation that need to be considered. How do we want to deal with a chronic if not yet terminal illness? How do we prepare for an ending, while years away from it?

Let's emphasize in bold type that **we do not think anyone else can determine what your quality of life is, or should be.** Many people who are chronically ill as well as many who live with a disability think their quality of life is fine. In fact, a number of surveys, as reported in medical journals, have found little or no differences between people living with a physical disability and those who were not when asked to rate life satisfaction, frustration with life, and mood. The important thing is to remember that most people adjust well to many different kinds of life stressors, and quality of life, after all, is what each of us defines it to be for ourselves.

Talking about It

If, like most Americans, you aren't prepared for chronic and terminal illnesses, the likelihood is that you haven't done enough thinking and talking about these matters.

If you don't think and talk about illness and dying, if you deny your mortality, that mortality becomes more frightening by the moment. And the longer you deny it, the less you will want to talk about it. You will continue to "refuse" to leave your friends, lovers, and family, or for them to leave you.

But we're here to tell you that acknowledgment of potential loss may be a better antidote against the poisonous loss itself than denial is; that learning to say good-bye may be a better way of dealing with loss than fearing to say good-bye; that learning how to stay in charge of what does or does not happen to you twenty or thirty years down the line may free you to make those last years and months fruitful.

Doesn't that make it a time to speak?

We need people to be asking questions—How do you treat pain? What will you do about my symptoms? At what point do you refer to hospice? Is there a palliative care service available in this hospital? I absolutely believe that as soon as consumers come to expect a higher level of care, then medical systems will find a way to provide that care.
—Betty Ferrell, R.N., Ph.D.

Sure, mortality still has its sting. Dying is and always will be a frightening prospect. But we can make our serious illnesses and our dying less frightening. We can make our older years less painful. And we can make the deaths of our loved ones emotionally and spiritually more fruitful.

When you have a serious illness, it is not the time to yield to others the right to make of it what they will. You should have choices at each important juncture in your life, at every turning point, and the end of life is certainly one of those junctures. In addition to what technological care you do and don't want, there is a wide range of other choices. To have choices become realities, you have to think and talk about these matters and write your decisions down, and then talk about them again until they are just like any other decisionmaking process in life.

Regarding death, Shakespeare has Hamlet say that "the readiness is all." He is talking about the preparedness of the spirit and the mind as well as of the body. That kind of preparedness takes work. But it's well worth it.

So change how you approach serious illness. Don't think of it as a terminal matter, but as a living matter.

Enter with us into this foreign country. In the pages that follow we will explain the rules of the road, explore the danger signs, the detours, the potholes. And we will suggest paths around these hazards.

4

PALLIATIVE CARE

Getting Pain and Suffering
Under Control

You need to know what your choices and opportunities are. In this chapter we talk about the rapidly changing world of what's called palliative care: taking care of the entire person—emotionally, physically, and spiritually—wherever and whenever he or she is seriously ill. Strictly speaking, palliative care can—and should—accompany attempts to save or prolong life; in practice, it often fills the gap between aggressive curative treatments and the end-of-life services offered by hospice programs (see chapter 5).

Palliative care is a cornerstone for dealing not only with terminal illnesses, but with chronic ones that may plague you for a decade or more before you reach the end of your life.

Palliative care addresses the pain and suffering that human beings are heir to, which is why the mantra of palliative care is: "*Sometimes* a cure is possible; but almost always we can *heal* a patient and the family." But that's not all, as Russel K. Portenoy, M.D., director of the Beth Israel Hospital Palliative Care Unit in New York City, explains:

> Good palliative care not only relieves symptoms and offers practical assistance for patients and caregivers in the home, it encourages discussion about values and decisions in planning for medical care, and respects these decisions after they are made. And, at the end of life, it offers opportunities for closure—even growth—and helps the bereaved deal with loss.

Before describing this important component of medical care in detail, a few words about the use of palliative care in our medical system. In a nation-wide study a few years ago, it was found that too many patients approaching the end of their lives had too many unpleasant or dangerous symptoms that weren't being addressed properly.

- Two-thirds of patients found that their physical or emotional symptoms were difficult to tolerate. These rates were not restricted to patients with cancer or in intensive care units.
- Shortness of breath affected most patients, 80 percent had severe fatigue, and 62 percent had debilitating emotional symptoms.
- The same survey reveals that patient depression remains one of the greatest end-of-life treatment challenges. Clinical depression is an issue for 40 percent of dying patients; half of the oncologists in the study did not feel competent to meet their patients' needs in this area.
- Many physicians appear to be uninformed about how patients can benefit from pain medications. Despite saying they felt competent to manage pain, up to 25 percent did not provide optimal pain management.

To combat this unpleasant picture, medical educational institutions and individual reformers have been pushing for the incorporation of palliative care into all modes of treatment and all kinds of institutions. And that's beginning to work.

So while medical schools and nursing schools have always trained to *cure* (i.e., treat the disease), in the last half decade they are also being used as training grounds for *healing* (i.e., treating emotional suffering and physical symptoms). Medical and nursing textbooks are adding lessons on pain management and care near the end of life.

Some have said that this is nothing more than a return to old-fashioned bedside care. But there's more to it than that. Health care personnel need to be shown how to acknowledge not just the patient's fears but the family's as well. They need to be given tools to alleviate anger. They need to be taught how to give up on their own guilt and denial when they can no longer cure.

Palliative care is actually a fairly recent addition to the store of weapons to deal with serious diseases, especially chronic ones. The hospice movement, which came from England in the late 1960s, has shown that looking after the "whole" person can improve quality of life enormously and, possibly, even extend life while a disease makes its way through a patient's system. This is a precious gift from abroad that was brought to us by a group of talented and persevering medical personnel, social workers, and clergy.

Palliative care is interdisciplinary. It aims to relieve suffering and improve quality of life. It strives to strengthen relations between you and your loved ones. It tries to make meaning out of meaninglessness. It helps prepare you for what's coming. Through bereavement counseling, it helps deal with the inevitable when it does happen.

Quality of Life

This is an important term in the new world of care. What does it connote? Among other things, it means that *you* set the definition of how you want to live, how you want to deal with your pain or other symptoms, and how you want to die.

A June 2003 Op-Ed piece in the *New York Times,* "False Hope in a Bottle," told the story of one man whose terminally ill wife was given what he called "false hope" by physicians who tried drug after drug in an effort to give her "a few more months." The author of the piece would have preferred to see his wife spared this trial. But in reply letters, some readers suggested that while keeping people alive just for the sake of a few more days of being hooked up to tubes was cruel, it is too easy to say that all such efforts are useless. In fact, some of the writers told stories of people whose minds were alive and active, while their bodies were not, or where last-minute interventions provided both time and quality.

And in rebuttal of those stories, one or two letter-writers told about their loved ones who, given a chance to deal with their spiritual rather than their physical health, arrived at the end "with dignity and peace."

In short, while delaying death may not be the same as prolonging life, each of us needs to decide which is which for ourselves.

Serious Illness

At what point would you consider that how you live your life is as important as getting your illness under control? Is there *any* point at which that would be so?

At what point do you want to choose *not* to go to the hospital for one more try at cure? Is there ever a point at which you would do that? What *do* you want to do? Go home? Be with friends? Travel? Go to the hospital only in an emergency or for special reasons?

In the Hospital

Do you want to be sedated so that you don't feel any pain, even if it means you can't communicate with your family? Do you want your health care providers to take responsibility to see that your life is as good as they can possibly get it, to continue to vary treatments and medicines, and to have conversations with you to help you deal with the problems you encounter during your illness?

Palliative care is a concept that offers many promises and opportunities, but also many dilemmas. Still, its promise is remarkable: opportunities for "a good death," and many possibilities to let us live more fully with serious or terminal illnesses, to make things come out right. When palliative care is available in a hospital and its specialists are called in because a patient is having trouble breathing, or is in physical, emotional, or spiritual pain, or a family needs information or support, wonderful things can happen.

Experts agree that the team for palliative care should include not only doctors and nurses, but social workers, psychologists, pharmacists, clergy, volunteers, and family members, and that doctors and nurses should be trained in the specialty.

Physical Comfort

There are many kinds of physical discomfort when people are ill, and palliative care experts are learning how to address all of them—vomiting, shortness of breath, diarrhea, and so forth—but pain is certainly among the worst.

Pain

From time immemorial, pain has been the bane of mankind. We now have the knowledge and treatments to assess and relieve most pain. Too frequently, however, we use neither this knowledge nor available treatments, and pain remains tragically undertreated.

- An estimated 50 million Americans suffer from chronic pain, but only 26 percent are referred to proper specialists. Fifty percent have their pain inadequately managed in their last days of life.
- Twenty-six percent of nursing home residents who reported daily pain received no medicine for it.
- More than 75 percent of patients with advanced cancer experience pain, yet cancer pain can be relieved for up to 90 percent of patients.
- Women are more likely than men to experience and seek help for pain. Yet they are less likely than men to be taken seriously and have their pain adequately treated.
- The situation is worse in the African American community.
- The negative effects of pain cost an estimated $100 billion each year.

Researchers at the Center for Gerontology and Health Care Research at Brown University (who did one of the studies on pain) stated, "There is no acceptable excuse for not treating pain appropriately in terminally ill patients."

Which, among other reasons, is why the Joint Commission on Accreditation of Healthcare Organizations—the major regulating body for hospitals in the United States—issued a 2001 document making pain the "fifth vital sign" in hospitals.

In other words, this highly respected commission, which accredits hospitals and health care providers throughout the country, now directs health care providers to assess, monitor, and treat pain as frequently as they monitor pulse, blood pressure, temperature, and respiration, and to:

- Properly assess the level of pain for all patients
- Recognize patients' rights to assess and help manage their own pain
- Track patients' complaints of pain and regularly reassess and follow up on those complaints
- Train the staff in pain assessment and management
- Support the appropriate prescribing of pain medications
- Educate patients and families about pain management
- Provide pain management instruction, medication, and other assistance when patients are discharged

And why is it so important to control pain? Not just because it's unpleasant, but because it gets in the way of all sorts of opportunities to make use of your final years, months, and days. Here, for instance, is what Dr.

Stephen Pantilat of the University of California Medical School in San Francisco has to say about that:

> People who are dying have lots of things that they want to take care of. They want to say good-bye to their loved ones. They want to finish writing a book. They want to enjoy the time they have. And pain really grips the mind and doesn't let go, it doesn't allow you to focus on the things that are, frankly, much more important than thinking about how much pain you're in.

And here's another famous palliative care specialist, Dr. Richard Payne at Duke University's Institute on Care at the End of Life: "There's a very practical issue of treating pain so that people can, in fact, get on with living the rest of their life while they're dying."

The Myths about Pain Control

Some doctors may feel it is "too soon" in a patient's illness to prescribe strong (opioid) medication, or they may fear they will hasten a patient's death if large doses are needed to control pain. Or, as Ira Byock, author of *Dying Well*, says:

> Many physicians react with frustration, annoyance, and then suspicion when a patient's pain doesn't rapidly improve, even when that person is dying. In the din of the strained health care system, the plaintive cries of the pained are faint indeed. It is high time we bring the same commitment of science and medical prowess to bear in treating chronic pain and improving the quality of life's end that we insist upon in oncology, cardiology and intensive care.

One of the traditional reasons that many physicians have historically been loath to administer enough powerful morphine and other such government-controlled substances is fear that patients might become addicted to them. In one report, concern over possible legal issues prompted 71 percent of New York State physicians to choose a weaker, less effective medication to avoid prescribing controlled substances.

It turns out that this fear is totally without foundation. According to Dr. Leigh Fredholm, "Patients who take pain medication for pain become more functional—they go to work; they interact with their families; they get out of bed; and they become more like themselves. In contrast, patients who take pain medications to get high become less functional—they go to bed; they lie; they cheat; they steal and become less like themselves." In other words, addiction and pain control are worlds apart.

Unfortunately, the issue is surrounded by ignorance, generated by the culture's instinctive fears of drug abuse. In 2001, a physician in California was sued for not prescribing *enough* opioid painkillers for his patient. A California jury awarded $1.5 million under a law that prohibits elder abuse. In the lawsuit, William Bergman's children sued their father's doctor, alleging that the physician was reckless in not prescribing strong enough medication for Bergman's severe pain. Bergman, who suffered from lung cancer, was admitted to the hospital on February 16, 1998, complaining of intolerable pain. He spent five days in the hospital and was discharged to die at home, still in agony. His family ultimately consulted another physician who prescribed proper pain medication, and Mr. Bergman finally obtained relief. The eighty-five-year-old retired railroad employee died in hospice care on February 24, 1998. A suit against the hospital was settled out of court. As part of that settlement, the hospital agreed to provide pain management classes to its staff and its doctors.

The press carried stories about the case and put physicians on notice that they had to consider pain palliation as an important part of their care—under penalty of the law. Other cases of this sort are now being dealt with by the courts.

As we started to write this book, a scandal about Oxycontin surfaced in the newspapers and on television. This powerful prescription time-release painkiller was being diverted from its intended purposes and abused. As a consequence, law enforcement agents were increasing their efforts to diminish its diversion and abuse. Unfortunately, these efforts led to physicians and pharmacists becoming afraid to dispense Oxycontin and other powerful painkillers for fear of being prosecuted for supplying addicts. Fortunately, the next chapter of this story is a happy one. Using its existing relationship with the Drug Enforcement Administration (DEA), Last Acts Partnership, with pain organizations, persuaded the agency to issue joint DEA–pain management organization statements to the medical and law-enforcement communities to reassure them that they would not be persecuted for legal, compassionate use of Oxycontin or other prescription drugs.

The Patient's Participation in Pain Control

The other side of any kind of medical care is what the patient does or does not want. If physicians have been loath to give strong pain medication, or poorly trained in how much is needed, patients are not far behind. A patient may suffer in silence because he thinks it is a character flaw to express pain, because he is afraid of addiction, or because he doesn't want to "bother" his doctor or distract her from other treatment. Some cultural issues also apply. In some ethnic communities, admitting pain or asking for help for it can be seen as a diminishment of character.

None of this should stand in the way of pain control. Among other things, these days it's not painful to get pain medication. It can be administered through patches and gels and drinks, so that needles often aren't necessary. And if an intravenous drip of morphine is called for, it can be attached to a pump that allows the patient to actually give himself a little dose *before* the pain gets too bad.

Two stories about pain control illustrate the two sides of this matter. The events occurred only three years apart, but are worlds apart in expertise and attitude.

Gerald A. woke one morning to find that he had terrible pain in his testicles. Fearing testicular cancer, he went to a urologist. The diagnosis was epididymitis, a painful but not terribly serious ailment, though it can last for years. The urologist prescribed hot baths and aspirin. These did not diminish Gerald's pain. His internist suggested some other medications— Tylenol, anti-inflammatories, Celebrex, Vioxx. With each medication, Gerald suffered from irritation either in his stomach or lower abdomen, and the drugs had no real effect upon his constantly-growing testicular pain.

Finally, after six months, and in desperation, Gerald went to the Internet to seek help. There he encountered another man who had this painful ailment. He told Gerald that he had found relief at a major hospital in New York City in a palliative care unit. Gerald went there. A physician well trained in palliative medicine gave him a single dose of Percocet, an opioid. For the first time in six months, Gerald found complete relief from his pain. He asked the physician in charge why his other doctors had not thought about such a simple solution.

"Most doctors aren't trained in pain relief," the physician replied. "They are afraid to overuse drugs."

Gerald went home with a supply of Percocet. He went back to the Internet to look it up. "Be careful," the Internet article said, "Percocet is a powerful opioid." In a panic, Gerald e-mailed the physician who had prescribed the drug. Reassuringly, she e-mailed back: "Do not worry. If you are taking the drug for pain, you will not become addicted."

Gerald took the drug for a few days, then, pain-free, stopped taking it. Two years later, he was still pain-free.

Lukas's Story

When I went back to the hospital for an operation related to my cancer, in the middle of writing this book, I was startled to see the changes in approaches to pain. Previously, no one had mentioned pain to me: it was assumed that if I had some, I'd let the physicians or nurses know. In fact, at one point during radiation in 1992, my throat hurt so much I had to make an emergency visit to the hospital to get some medication. No one had brought this up as a possibility, and no one had asked about pain during my entire treatment.

This time, however, *everyone* asked about pain.

It was one of the vital signs they checked for when I first came for an interview with the surgeon, and at every point during my six-day hospital stay. When I said I had pain, they asked for a rating on a scale from 1 to 10.

Many times the nurses reminded me that it was better to "get ahead of the pain," using intravenous opioids, than to wait until it hit hard.

In fact, I was so impressed with the attention to pain as a factor in care that I remarked on it to several friends.

Once I had been operated upon and lay in the hospital bed, an intravenous drip delivered pain medication every half-hour directly to the nerves in my back, rather than to my bloodstream (the old way). In addition, should I have "breakthrough" pain (a sudden surge in pain), I could push a button and a device would pump a small jolt of medication on top of the half-hourly dose. This was limited: I could do it only every ten minutes.

Boy, I thought, they've put this pain control stuff into full throttle!

The only thing no one thought to ask was whether I was getting *too much* pain relief.

I had so much medication that I had double vision. I couldn't talk straight. I couldn't read, and I couldn't watch TV. My wife and children found me too drowsy to carry on a conversation. I slept a lot. It occurred to me that if I were dying and my family came to have a last conversation with me, I would be unable to do so.

In other words, pain control, wonderful as it was, should be balanced with other tools of palliative care. Someone should have monitored my ability to communicate with loved ones, my ability to function as I might want to function.

The second day after the operation, I asked them to withdraw the intravenous pump, to give me pills at night if I couldn't sleep. Gradually I regained some control of my eyesight, my tongue, and my brain.

But, it was wonderful knowing that someone was concerned about my pain, that they addressed it long before it became a problem. Knowing what I had to face, they asked questions so that I could be informed and make choices without fear of being told I was "wrong." Over and over I heard, "If you change your mind later, that's fine. We can always go back to the pain pump."

So pain control, while possible, is not the only thing to strive for in palliative care. Communication between the patient and those around him is also terribly important.

Lukas reports that other aspects of palliative care were neglected. His mental state, for instance. He wasn't just over-medicated; he was also depressed by his inability to get up, have good food, and go on with his life, not to mention the predictions that it would take him six months to feel like himself again. But his nurses were not interested in his mental state. Good palliative care provided by palliative care specialists should monitor and address more than physical pain.

Other Physical Symptoms

Almost from the start of any kind of treatment for serious illness or disease, patients can experience discomfort that ranges from the relatively minor (being tired or short of breath, dry mouth, difficulty swallowing, nausea) to more severe (weakness, confusion, outright pain.) As long as patients are willing to bring up these symptoms with their physicians, or the nurses notice them, there is no reason why they cannot be addressed, and that, too, is one of palliative care's goals.

The tools that exist to deal with these are myriad, ranging from medications to massage to music, from art therapy to pet therapy, from acupuncture to aromatherapy, from medical to chiropractic.

The Role of Nurses in Palliative Care

Giving relief to patients is generally thought of as being the realm of physicians. But, in fact, it is often nurses who have the most contact with a patient. Hospital nurses tend the sick on a round-the-clock basis. It is often nurses who have the time to chat with patients about their overall condition and problems. They give routine care and ask the not-so-routine questions. And as managed health care organizations have cut down the amount of time that physicians can spend with individual patients, it is nurses (either as R.N.s or nurse practitioners or hospice nurses) who ask about family, about emotional states, about general matters that impinge on good care.

The American Nursing Association's Web site has a strong statement about this:

> One of the major concerns of dying patients and their families is the fear of intractable pain during the dying process. Indeed, overwhelming pain can cause sleeplessness, loss of morale, fatigue, irritability, restlessness, withdrawal, and other serious problems for the dying patient. Nurses play an extremely important role in the assessment of symptoms and the control of pain in dying patients because they often have the most frequent and continuous patient contact.

Emotional and Spiritual Comfort

Human emotions take off on a wild ride after diagnosis of a major disease, falling under the general rubric of *suffering*. These can range from depression to anxiety to anger—or include all of these at once. People ask deep questions of themselves, such as, Was my life worth it? and What's the meaning of it all? These are powerful and moving questions that demand to be answered.

Good palliative care, begun early enough, can help you and your family: by fostering hope where it makes sense; by helping emotionally with psychotherapy or other counseling; by countering with a dose of reality when depression or fear exaggerates the state or stage of a disease.

Good palliative care can be a tremendous aid in giving you hope, reducing fear, alleviating depression and anxiety, and putting the world in greater perspective—in short, alleviating spiritual distress.

Taken in its entirety, the purpose of palliative care is to enhance quality of life, for you *and* for your family. Fear of loss of control, fear of the unknown, reduction of the ability to function in the world—all of this makes for a poorer quality of life, as do pain and other physical discomforts.

The range of tools that are now being brought to bear on both physical and emotional discomfort are many. For instance, there are so-called "adjunct" therapies—sometimes called "alternative medicine," sometimes "complementary medicine." At Memorial Sloan-Kettering Cancer Center in New York City, for instance, the Integrative Medicine Service offers yoga, meditation, massage, and tai chi, among others, in a rich package:

- Touch therapies
- Mind–body therapies
- Movement therapies
- Nutritional and herbal counseling

One of the newest and most interesting therapies is laughter. Yes, laughter. Even in the middle of serious illness, it turns out that people can laugh. And some experts believe that laughter not only can relieve people of having to constantly think about their illness or their pain, but can actually *cure* illness.

Lukas's Story _____

When I got lymphoma for the first time, I was getting radiation every day for five weeks. It was still quite frightening to me, since I didn't know whether it would be successful or not. At home, we ate well, had friends over, and watched comedy shows. It wasn't a normal habit of mine, but the English version of *Whose Line Is It Anyway?* had just started running every night on the Comedy Channel, and my wife and I found it hilarious. Whether it did anything for my lymphoma, I have no way of knowing, but it sure healed the spirit!

Now, eleven years later, with my lymphoma returning and me lying in the hospital for six days after my operation, I'm desperately bored. Then my wife notices that the hospital is having a comedy performance at 3:00 P.M. She urges us to go. It's just down the hall, in the arts and crafts room. "Oh, sure," I exclaim, "that's going to be a lot of fun. You think Sloan-Kettering has great comedians just lurking in the hallways? Besides, I won't be able to enjoy it with all the pain I'm having from walking around."

How wrong I was, on every count. Joining about twenty other patients—the young, the old, the halt; those with catheters and IV pumps; those already ambulatory, like myself—and their families, we sat waiting for "the comedians."

A young woman introduced herself. "My name is Abby Russell. I'm the founder of the Hamptons Comedy Festival. My mission is to both celebrate comedy arts and to use comedy to help fight cancer."

Fight cancer! Come on, I say to myself; who believes that stuff?

Ms. Russell went on to tell us that she thinks of comedy the way she thinks of any other influence on our immune systems: if painkillers or psychotherapy or music can make us less stressed, and if less stress means our immune system will be less compromised, then maybe, just maybe, our bodies can fight our disease a little more productively.

The first comic shows up. He has huge ears, almost like the ears of Santa Claus's elves, and he waits for a long time for the laughs after each joke. The jokes are actually good. There's the airplane joke, the Elvis Presley joke, the joke about the man who's so thin his pajamas have only one stripe.

The laughs come slowly at first, then more and more energetically. I realize that I'm laughing because my stomach hurts like crazy (laughter, coughs, and sneezes are *not* recommended for abdominal surgery patients!), but I can't help myself.

And when it's over, I realize that for one solid hour I have not thought for an instant about cancer or my iffy future. I haven't even minded the pain.

Whether it's morphine or one's family, or Reiki massage or acupuncture, or comedy, addressing the wide range of emotional and spiritual problems that patients experience upon diagnosis and when they're being treated, palliative care can help. Medical personnel need to be aware of these emotions and be prepared to help the patient with them.

Take one of the more problematic reactions as discussed by Dr. Linda Emanuel of EPEC:

Symptoms take on a life of their own and people build up responses to symptoms. So if I have a good deal of pain I am likely to build up a good deal of anxiety about having pain, and many associations with that pain. Or if I have nausea with chemotherapy, I will build up associations with the place that I had chemotherapy, or the person who gave me chemotherapy, and I won't be able to see that place or person without feeling nauseous. Those are normal, physical responses that connect to our psyche and our emotions. So if you can control the symptoms early, you avoid those associations. And if you can't control the symptoms at least you can know about the associations and the responses and try and find some other way of approaching those, because they become problems in themselves.

Palliative care provides powerful medicine when necessary, to combat physical pain. For emotional pain, it provides counseling and support. For spiritual pain, it offers a sympathetic ear to listen to your needs.

Palliative care affirms life and regards dying as a natural process that is a profoundly personal experience for the individual and family. Palliation enables patients to function and communicate with loved ones during the final months or days of a terminal illness, and early in the disease process as well. (More about that in a few pages.) Palliative care comforts the patient and the family, ensuring that the last months and days of life can be carried on in as normal a fashion as possible. In terms of spiritual relief, at the end of life, palliative care can be used to bring you and your family together, and to give bereavement care after your death.

It is, as we said, a powerful concept. While it demands enormous changes in the medical system, many are already under way.

Palliative Care from the Provider's Point of View

What does this new way of care and this new way of thinking about care mean to those delivering it?

Here are a few words from some leading providers in the field.

Leigh Fredholm, M.D.: "What we seek to do is relieve pain and physical symptoms and let patients do whatever it is they want to do with their time—without having to be concerned with physical problems."

Patricia Neely, M.D.: "In my experience, good palliative medicine demands an intensity that rivals what goes on in an ICU."

J. Dudley Youman, M.D.: "I don't think there are many physicians who want to carry on beyond the point where there is a reasonable expectation of a benefit from extreme measures. When we reach that point, we can go into a mode where we are looking at comfort and supportive measures instead of the ICU and more tubes, which won't really going to change the ultimate outcome."

Charles Von Gunten, M.D.: "Achieving a good death is an important and rewarding part of medical care. Physicians need to see that this is possible. That it's not a diminution of their skills. Participating in good end-of-life care does not mean being a poor physician, or not being a scientific physician. If anything, it is the culmination of all the aspirations of a physician."

Neil Stone, M.D.: "A doctor who can be there for a patient, even at the end, can empower people."

Finally, there's the story of Janice Mulder, M.D., a traditionally trained doctor who discovered the benefits to her patients and to herself of working in palliative care:

As a physician, I was trained to investigate the problem, make the diagnosis and prescribe the treatment. What happens when I can't fix the problem and there is nothing I can do to make it go away?

I was taught that doctors were not supposed to feel. We needed to keep a good objective distance between our patients and ourselves. If I admitted that I was having problems, I would be labeled as a weak physician and someone who couldn't cope.

It became apparent that this rift within myself, the inner wound that occurred during my medical training, caused a large part of my distress. I needed to heal that rift and claim my work as a whole physician. It has taken me time to discover how I need to practice palliative medicine and to stand firm in my own conviction.

So, what is it that I offer my patients and their families? My expertise as a physician is crucial in my ability to help make people physically comfortable, and I am currently expanding my own definition of what it means to be a responsive physician. Pain and suffering are often exacerbated by psycho-spiritual distress. I have had to come to my own understanding of the meaning of life and death. I have been challenged to reach beyond my ability to prescribe drugs, to be willing to be fully present with my patients and their families, and to use myself as an instrument as I have journeyed with them. A high degree of self-awareness is needed so that I can sort out what is mine and what belongs to my patients.

When one forms authentic relationships the caring that one gives is returned. It is a two-way street. My work in palliative medicine has facilitated my own inner healing.

—from *Healing the Rift Within: Confessions of a
Palliative Care Physician*

Moving Palliative Care "Upstream"

As if the changes already in place were not momentous enough, there is a push to take the tools of palliative care that are used for dying people and move them "upstream," that is, closer to the time of diagnosis of serious ailments, for use with people who are nowhere near close to dying. Michael Preodor, M.D., explains the thinking behind this concept:

If you look at the tools that the palliative care specialist has developed, we have a remarkable ability to control pain. We also have some pretty good tools for nausea. A little bit for fatigue and weakness. A lot for skin care. Those tools should be used any time during illness, not just for the patient who has just a few months to live. You get nauseous with your chemotherapy, even though you're not anywhere near death; in fact you're hoping still for cure, or at least significant life prolongation. You still should have the nausea controlled.

I think what's also a key to what we've learned in palliative medicine is communication. Anyone who has to face decisions about therapies ought to be able to know exactly what the chances of success are, to know every side effect and to make a pretty informed decision. We should know how to break bad news and how to help somebody make good decisions.

Summing Up

Here's what you may want to remember:

- Palliative care appreciates that dying, while a normal process, is a critical period in the life of the patient and family, and responds aggressively to the associated human suffering while acknowledging the potential for personal growth.
- It places a high priority on physical comfort and functional capacity, including, but not limited to, expert management of pain and other symptoms, diagnosis and treatment of psychological distress, and assistance in remaining as independent as possible or desired.
- It provides physical, psychological, social, and spiritual support to help the patient and family adapt to the anticipated decline associated with an advanced, progressive, incurable disease.
- It extends support beyond the life span of the patient to assist the family in their bereavement, among other things. For instance, in the past, families had "visiting hours," and the emphasis was on patient care alone. Now families are more likely to be welcome at the bedside all the time, as palliative care promotes patient function, but also looks to help the family through this crisis, not only during illness, but long afterward.
- It provides concrete supportive services to caregivers such as respite,

round-the-clock availability of expert advice and support by telephone, grief counseling, personal care assistance, and referral to community resources.

- It recognizes and addresses the economic costs of caregiving, including loss of income and nonreimbursable expenses.

In developing a plan of care, a pain management strategy that incorporates the patient's wishes and needs must be included.

If you or someone you know is in pain, whether they're in a hospital setting or nursing home, ask—on the spot—for a palliative care consultation.

You can also file a complaint with the Joint Commission on Accreditation of Healthcare Organizations (JCAHO) on the quality of care received at any healthcare organization they accredit. Complaint information is used to strengthen JCAHO oversight activities and to improve the quality of care in accredited facilities. JCAHO will address complaints relating to issues regarding patient rights, care of patients, safety, infection control, medication use, and security.

5

THE FACTS ABOUT HOSPICE

Our health care system puts most of its energy and money into cure and, where end-of-life matters are concerned, into aggressive treatment.

For many people, this is a good thing.

For some, it's not.

If you consider the quality-of-life issues we've discussed, there is more to living than mere survival. As Anna Moretti, a nurse and hospice administrator, says, "The spiritual side, the psychological side, and certainly the social side are not being addressed."

Most patients still die in hospitals, many of them in intensive care units that control their breathing, their ingestion of nutrition, and everything else. Moretti puts it this way: "ICUs are set up so that you have 10 minutes to visit with your family member an hour. I recently visited a couple who had been married for over 45 years. The husband got 10 minutes an hour to spend with his wife. And she was dying. And the family knew that, the doctor knew that, the nurse knew that. Yet they were unwilling to change the rules for that visitation. In hospice, there's never a limit."

Hospice—that's what this chapter is about. Hospice is where the concept of palliative care is put to work 100 percent. In fact palliative care, as described in the last chapter, was born in a hospice setting. Here's how it worked for Ruth Wolf.

For eleven years, Ruth waged a fierce battle against cancer. At the age of fifty-eight, she had gone through chemotherapy, attended cancer support groups, researched new cancer treatments, challenged her oncologist's decisions, and endured both a double mastectomy and a bone marrow transplant. When the cancer spread to her brain, she decided it was time to die. Ruth wanted to exert as much control over the course of her dying as she had over her disease, and dying at home was paramount to that wish. With the help of hospice, her two extremely supportive daughters, and her husband, she was able to do just that. Ruth had her hospital bed and oxygen tank placed in her living room, so that her many friends would feel more comfortable visiting than if she were in her bedroom.

"She wasn't hiding," recalled her daughter Dagny. A multitude of friends came through—friends from childhood, from her college days, and from her cancer support group. "They had time to talk with her," Dagny said. "In fact, people would come and camp out in our house." For the two months before her death, the house was constantly filled with the sounds of laughter, talking, and ringing phones, just as Ruth had wanted.

"Mom had collected dozens of scarves to cover her head while she was in chemotherapy," Dagny said. "She had us drape the scarves over the furniture, and asked each visitor to take a scarf to have something to remember her by. When they chose a scarf, she told a story that went along with how she had bought that particular one. It's tragic that she died so young, but if we could all die like she did, we'd be fortunate. I take great pride in the fact that we helped her have the death that she wanted, and that she was able to do it at home."

Even though hospice—from the Latin word for hospitality—was originally designed as a *place* for people who were dying, it no longer means that. Hospice, as we know it today, is a way of giving care to people for whom aggressive medical treatments no longer offer a benefit, in a variety of settings: at home, in stand-alone hospice units, in nursing homes, in hospitals.

Let's be clear: hospice is about living. It is about seeing to it that people with a short or a long time to live—but without much hope of cure—can have good quality of life, can live well until the very moment of death.

To some of you, the notion of quality of life while dying may seem a contradiction. But to hundreds of thousands of others, it makes perfect sense. The number of people who are under hospice care—80 percent of them at home—has grown dramatically in the last few years, and the idea that hospice is just another word for giving you pain pills is disappearing. Hospice, in short, is an effort to come to terms with death on an existential and spiritual level, for patient *and* family.

Here's but one example:

Katherine Salansky lives with her husband Robert. They've been married for thirty-nine years and have five children. Fourteen years ago, she was diagnosed with Chronic Obstructive Pulmonary Disease (COPD).

"They said, 'You may have five years, you may have ten. At the most, fifteen.' Well, here I am fourteen years later, and I'm still running."

Katherine's condition has worsened. She's battled pneumonia many times, and has been in and out of the hospital. The doctors have told Katherine there is nothing more they can do; there is no cure for COPD. A lung transplant has been ruled out, and she now has end-stage lung disease.

"I'm on oxygen now." She says the slow progression of her disease has given her a lot of time to think about death. She says that at this stage quality of life is more important than quantity. In fact she has a DNR—a do-not-resuscitate order—hanging over her bed.

"Seeing what I've seen and learning what I've learned about death and dying and transplants and quality—I guess that's what I'm dealing with, quality. I don't want just to be kept alive."

For a long time, she didn't consider hospice care: "I think it was when the doctor said to me, 'Clinically, we don't know what's keeping you going, but I think you'd do well to talk to hospice,' that I knew how serious it was."

Katherine thought about it for a few days, but didn't call. It was her daughter who arranged an in-home visit. Now Katherine receives hospice care. She can't say enough about the care she receives, and says that by doing this interview, she hopes to change the way people feel about hospice.

"You say *hospice* to people, they put their heads down and won't look you in the eye. It's a fact. Even pharmacists are embarrassed. I guess it scares them. I say, Don't be embarrassed for me, 'cause I've got the best. I've got my primary doctor, I've got my nurses, my hospice, my family. I even have a little scooter I get around on. I can visit the neighbors if I want to. Hospice is helping me to get the best out of the life I have left."

What Hospice Can Do for You

If you can wrap your mind around the meaning of hospice, you can begin to take greater control of your physical and mental well-being during times of serious, life-threatening illness.

Let's say it again: Hospice is not simply about death, but rather about the quality of life as we wind down our lives. And it's for *all* concerned—patient, family, friends, as well as the health professional community itself.

It's been thirty-five years since the term hospice resurfaced. Used in the Middle Ages to mean a resting place for travelers, it was reinvented in the mid-twentieth century by a British physician's nurse (now a physician), Dame Cecily Saunders, as a place to take care of patients whose diseases had put them in too much pain or other discomfort to stay at home, and whose diseases were probably not open to cure, so no hospital really wanted them.

If, as we've suggested, some both in and outside the medical profession used to think of hospice as "a place to go when you're dying," more and more are beginning to think of it as a *concept:* that no person should be alone, or in pain, or separated from loved ones or from compassionate care when they are seriously ill or dying. And afterward, too: hospice habitually offers bereavement counseling for family and loved ones for a full year after death.

Hospice offers home nursing, home medical visits, help with medication, help lifting an ill patient; it offers respite care for exhausted home caregivers such as spouses or grown children. It supplies physical therapy, social workers, and—if necessary—inpatient care at a hospice inpatient unit or hospital. This is what is meant by *holistic care.*

Hospice, very simply, is a model for compassionate care at the end of life. It emphasizes pain and symptom management and psychological and spiritual support. This care is tailored to the needs and wishes of patients and their loved ones.

In 2001, approximately 2.4 million Americans died. Over seven hundred thousand of those Americans received hospice care. In other words, one out of every three Americans who died in the United States of all causes had some hospice care.

The bad news is that most of those who received hospice care did so for too little time to experience its full benefit. This is not only a waste of opportunity, it is totally unnecessary. Let's look at why this happens.

Why People Don't Use Hospice

No One Likes Bad News

Many doctors find it difficult to give bad news, and there are many patients who don't want to receive it.

Nurse and innovator Betty Ferrell says, "Primarily what I see is patients who come to hospice literally a few days to perhaps a week before they die. And the most common comment from patients and families is, why did nobody think of this sooner? Do you have any idea what it's been like for us the last six months?

If it weren't so sad, the manner in which this happens would be humorous. Moretti says that introducing hospice care would force doctors to break news to a family or patient that is unpleasant, so they don't want to do it. And the patient, believing that such news is an immediate death sentence, decides, If I avoid that determination, then I'll avoid death. Which prevents the patient and those around him from benefiting from hospice care. Moretti explains the all-too-common communication stalemate:

> I get a call from a family and the family doesn't understand why the physician didn't bring it up. When I call that physician, the physician says—I don't understand why the family doesn't bring this up. And so there's this collusion that takes place where there's a silence and they both believe if neither one brings it up, then it must not really be warranted. And this dance goes on and on. And it's something we hear about all the time.

"Hospice Is Only for Six Months"

Another barrier to utilization of hospice is a misconception on the part of both patients and practitioners that federal and private insurance will cover hospice benefits for no more than six months.

This has never been true. The Medicare hospice benefit actually requires that physicians make a best-guess estimate as to when the patient's disease— *if it takes a natural course*—would cause the patient to die within six months. But this is so difficult to predict that doctors are reluctant to make the guess. This reluctance—and patients' reluctance to hear bad news—kept usage of hospice down. There was a time when hospices actually were threatened with sanctions by Medicare if a patient lived *longer* than six months, though everyone should have been delighted if they did so!

Today hospice patients can be recertified to receive the hospice benefit over and over, as long as the patient is alive, and in the last few years, Medicare and the hospice industry have come to a much better understanding. If only physicians and patients and families knew it! In April 2002, the Center for Medicare and Medicaid Services (the federal agency in charge of these matters) issued a very important letter stating in no uncertain terms that Medicare, and in some cases Medicaid, does not limit payment to six months. Certainly, hospice care is available for far longer than the fourteen days that the average patient is now using it.

Hospice Makes Patients "Give Up"

Many fear that accepting hospice care is a self-fulfilling prophecy, that acknowledging a terminal condition speeds the disease process or that treatment stops. Moretti sets the record straight:

> Even though the goal is mainly to relieve the symptoms at hand, treatments don't stop. In fact, they can get more aggressive as we try to relieve all the symptoms that may be present in different types of disease states. And some of our patients do improve in our program. If you have a nurse visiting your home every other day to make sure you're taking your medications, or even to provide relief to your caregiver so they can get rest, then life becomes more social, and people have more of a will to participate in life.

The Truth about Hospice

Hospice care is self-defined, as Anna Moretti again explains:

> The goal of hospice care is whatever the patient says they would like it to be: For instance, to see to it that the patient's suffering is relieved, that they can live a quality of life that's acceptable to them, that the family is allowed to move on from their death.

1. Almost Everyone Can Benefit from Hospice

Cancer patients use hospice more than any others, because incurable cancer has a fairly predictable decline, at least in the end stage. However, many if not most cancers are actually chronic diseases, with many, many years of active and productive life for the patients.

But hospice care—and the practices that go with it—are useful for a much larger population. Patients with *end-stage* heart disease or in the advanced stages of ALS (Lou Gehrig's disease) and other chronic, long-term ailments are often unaware of hospice as a choice.

Increasing numbers of Americans—and their physicians—now recognize that much of the pain and sense of hopelessness that accompany terminal illness can be eased for millions of patients by hospice services designed specifically to help them; services that are covered by Medicare and private insurance companies when properly certified and appropriately managed; services where hopefully the health care system eliminates the bad choice between cure *or* palliative care.

Putting it another way, one hospice worker said, "Here's how I like to frame it for people. By adding support, by adding caregivers and expertise and more spiritual care, more physician care, nursing care, all of it, you become more able to do the things you want to do. The goal is to make sure that you're as highly functioning as possible through the good control of your symptoms."

2. Hospices Offer a Range of Services

- Medical and nursing care
- Medical equipment (such as wheelchairs or walkers)
- Pharmaceutical therapy for pain relief and symptom control
- Home health aide and homemaker services
- Social work services
- Physical and occupational therapy
- Speech therapy
- Spiritual care
- Diet counseling
- Bereavement and other counseling services
- Case management

3. Where to Find Hospice Care

Hospice at home has been the ideal model over the years. Having care in a familiar setting, where familiar people surround you, has a very soothing effect on patients. But all that may be changing. As Anna Moretti points out, "As families changed throughout the years, there have been fewer children in the home to help. There have been fewer caregivers available or people who could leave work to take care of their loved one. Sometimes we have an eighty-five-year-old woman taking care of her ninety-year-old husband. So the model has changed over the years."

In other words, more and more hospices have inpatient units, and nursing homes and hospitals will have to increase their use of hospice care.

Most inpatient hospices are used for acute crisis management of dying patients, but in-home hospice care is offered for all qualifying patients, no matter whether they are in the last stages of an illness or not.

4. How It Works

Hospice is delivered by a team approach: "There's no one team member who believes that what he or she is doing is more important than what the others bring to the care of that patient," says Moretti.

Team members include not only doctors, but also nurses, social workers, chaplains, assistants, and volunteers. The most important team member, according to hospice experts, is actually the patient and his or her family, for they lead the others in determining what care is needed and wanted. The rest of the team brings to that patient and to that family different types of care to relieve that patient's suffering. For most patients, this team stays the same throughout their care, which is one of the great blessings of hospice: whether inpatient or in the home, care is provided by a consistent team of people who know the patient and family, and whom the family knows. In contrast, anyone who has been to a hospital knows that the care team often rotates. You never quite know who you're getting!

5. Who Pays for Hospice?

In general, the answer is that Medicare pays for hospice care if you're over sixty-five. Private insurers pay for it if you're not, although private and government payers can work together, also, to pick up different costs.

The Medicare Benefit

If a patient needs palliative care and management of a terminal condition, and if a physician is able to state that this patient—in the normal course of this disease or ailment—will probably not live longer than six months, then:

The patient will be entitled to two initial ninety-day periods of hospice care and an unlimited number of sixty-day periods, as long as the doctor certifies at the beginning of each period that the individual's medical condition continues to decline and that he/she has a life expectancy of about six months, under normal conditions.

What this means is that the whole host of hospice services, in the home, in a stand-alone facility, or in a unit of another facility, are available and reimbursable through Medicare.

6. Family Participation

As we stated above, family is a large part of hospice care. In fact, the focus of hospice is not on the patient alone, but on patient and family as a unit. Hospitals have always had a difficult time including the family in the continuum of care. But since the hospice care team uses its expertise to involve family in the treatment of the patient, the family must also allow itself to be brought into the healing care of the hospice. New and rewarding things happen. Important relationships become reestablished. Important things get said. Buried secrets are unearthed. Loved ones begin to express their love in terms that prior life experience, the disease, or the dying process may have restricted.

"I think the more I observe families and patients while they're going through this process, the more I realize that everyone does it individually; that there is no one way of doing it well or correctly or right or wrong. And it amazes me, the grace and dignity that appears at these time periods," says Anna Moretti.

Here's a story about one family:

When a difficult decision had to be made about whether to proceed with a second course of brain radiation to treat the spread of the cancer, Maria C. had candid conversations with her physician that allowed her to weigh the advantages and disadvantages—the possibility of more fatigue, nausea, and headaches—against quality time with her husband. She decided against more radiation. Three months before her death, she entered a hospice program, remaining at home with regular visits from the hospice team. She died comfortably, her husband at her side. For her husband, looking back on his wife's long illness three weeks after her death, expert palliative care provided "an easing of tension, an easing of what people go through."

7. Hospitals Benefit from On-site Programs

There is another change in the hospice and hospital scene that may prove valuable. Because of the underutilization of hospice care, and because patients and family (as well as physicians) often hold off asking about hospice, hospitals are themselves beginning to have on-site hospices. These are much more than palliative care units; sometimes they are run as cooperative programs between hospitals and outside hospices.

Dr. Diane Meier, a palliative care specialist at Mt. Sinai Hospital in New York City who has written on the subject, suggests a number of reasons why this kind of in-hospital hospice unit is useful.

1. Because beginning physicians learn a great deal from their in-hospital internships, if palliative care, in general, and hospice, specifically, are present in hospitals, the young doctors can learn right from the beginning about these methods of care.
2. Since most communities in the United States have hospice programs, "Partnering gives hospitals access to an untapped repository of palliative care expertise as well as to integrated continuity of care for our most vulnerable patients and their families."

Meier suggests that Medicare costs would probably go down if in-hospital hospices are used, "since 5% of the dying are readmitted to hospital needlessly and they expend 30% of the health care dollar. Hospice options would cut these costs."

She also points out that "Partnerships allow hospices to be in touch with patients much earlier in their illnesses."

Hospice Caregivers

Who are these people who take care of you when you're seriously ill or dying? What kind of caregivers are they? Why would anyone want to spend day after day taking care of people at the end of their lives? Here are the voices of a few. It's very comforting to know that these are the kinds of people who will be looking after us.

As a chaplain for hospice, I help people who have terminal illness, as well as their families. My role can take several forms. And the basic idea behind the role is one of presence, to help alleviate some of the loneliness. There are a few ways that we do that. One way is simply the act of being with the family or the person with the life-limiting illness. Another way is to connect the family or the person with their own spiritual tradition—finding them clergy or a congregation that they might gain comfort from. And the third role is to actually help them explore—be present during their exploration of—spiritual questions and concerns.

—Melissa Hart, hospice chaplain

Dying people have a lot of issues to resolve; my goal is for people to be able to die peacefully. We can't make good deaths but we can make better deaths. We don't have profound enough things to say, but we can be sure there's someone standing with them.

—Edwina Taylor, R.N., hospice innovator

I think ultimately we're realizing that good hospice care should be the same as good medical care generally, and vice versa. What we've been doing in hospice we should be doing for everyone who is ill, whether they're dying or whether they are not. Care is about the whole person when it works well.

—Linda Emanuel, M.D.

In the Field

If patients' and doctors' perception of hospice may not be changing fast enough, it is still changing. In 1991 about 170,000 people used hospice care. Ten years later, over half a million were using it. That's a huge increase in the sheer number of people using the services. And the figure continues to rise.

What's more, there are a lot of planners, ethicists, and government officials talking about the benefits of hospice and how they can be expanded. We're going to tell you about just one of the many discussions.

In 2003, the Hastings Center, an ethics think tank of long standing and eminent reputation, got together with the National Hospice Work Group to figure out how to make the flexible and professional activities of hospice organizations available to more and more people—not in order to hasten people into a mode of dying, but to take what hospice has to offer and make it available earlier and earlier, in chronic illnesses as well as terminal conditions.

The reason the group decided to do this was because for those who get to use hospice and come in contact with hospice organizations, the quality of care is so much superior to general care for seriously ill people that the writers of this report (Access to Hospice Care: Expanding Boundaries, Overcoming Barriers) wanted more Americans to have access to it.

Here's just some of what they had to say:

1. Hospice is beneficial because like its partner palliative care, it "offers the best possible quality of life for patients and their families."
2. "Hospices are rich and complex in virtually all their facets—in the skills and services they provide, in the needs they meet, in the expectations that people have of them."
3. Hospice should be "not for the imminently dying only, but for those wrestling with the complex clinical and personal decisions associated with an eventually fatal illness."
4. Society has an obligation to "provide health care equitably," and that goes for end-of-life care, too.
5. But it's not happening. "Persons who may actually live longer than six months can significantly benefit from hospice services. A person may not need every service that a hospice can provide all at once, but over time . . . special aspects of hospice care are very important to a given individual." However, because of the "six-month rule," fear of talking about death and dying, and the perception of what hospice is ("giving up"), many dying persons never get referred to hospice; others come only in the very final days; and cultural differences contribute to great underuse.
6. Finally, the writers agreed that hospice organizations are so well geared to flexible and dynamic change, to developing new expertise and

services to meet changing needs, that they should be given more opportunity to serve a greater and greater community. For instance, they should be given the lead role in developing palliative care "across the healthcare spectrum."

The full report is too long to include, even in an appendix, but here are its final recommendations. They represent a powerful dream for the future of care for those facing chronic life-limiting illnesses over a long time, as well as for those nearing the end of life.

1. "Healthcare leaders, policymakers, and others must come to consensus on the definition of palliative care and develop a framework for greater accountability in palliative care delivery."
2. "Public policy should expand the scope of hospice services."
3. "Expand access and delivery of hospice to dying persons residing in long-term care facilities" (nursing homes).
4. "Leaders . . . must promote hospice–hospital partnerships in order to meet the current and projected needs of the rapidly expanding volume of chronically and terminally ill patients."
5. "Develop educational programs to 'reintroduce' hospice and palliative care to the public in light of their new capabilities, flexibility, and accessibility."

Given the speed with which palliative care and hospice have moved in the past thirty years, the above recommendations and vision may not be out of the question, but vast sums of money and goodwill are needed to make them happen.

6

THE ABCS OF ADVANCE DIRECTIVES

There is no way around the reality of death and dying. But Americans are learning that end-of-life conversations can be a pathway leading them to a better way of dying. The end of life, say experts, need not be all angst and agony, but a time of surprising personal growth.

—from www.findingourway.net

S o, now what? How do you get around the obstacles, choose your goals for care, learn to communicate with your physician, and get what you want when you're ill? A tall order? Yes, indeed. But not an impossible one to fill.

You may not have heard the term *advance directives* before. It's a very important part of this book, one that covers two main types of documents: the living will and the medical power of attorney. Before you can create these binding documents describing how you want to be cared for when you can't speak for yourself, you'll need to think and talk to trusted confidants about what, exactly, you want.

Identifying Your Priorities

Perhaps you will want to begin with a conversation with yourself, in your head. Perhaps you have seen relatives die or heard stories about people who used their last years or months or days to great advantage. Maybe you know someone who was kept alive by artificial means too long, or someone who pulled the plug before you would have done so. Maybe you haven't wanted to face any of these issues, but now that a relative is dying or you yourself are ill, they have to be faced.

Or just maybe you're able to think about these issues at a younger age—say, fifty—and you understand the value of doing so. Whatever your reason, there are questions worth posing to yourself (and to those you love). From the experience of those who have grappled with such questions, we can say that you will find the end of life much, much easier, closer to what you would want for yourself, if you do ask yourself such questions as:

- Where do you want to spend your last days, weeks, months?
- Who do you want to speak for you if you can no longer make decisions for yourself—not just when you're dying, but any time you are too ill to make health care decisions?
- What do you want your caretakers to do about pain, artificial nutrition, and fluids?
- Under what circumstances do you want health professionals to do "everything" they can to keep you alive, and under what circumstances do you not want them to do so? Do you want to be resuscitated, or do you want a DNR ("do not resuscitate" order) in your chart?
- Have you thought about what financial preparations need to be made, and how you will pay for a long-term serious illness?

Of course, none of this will be totally new to you. By the time you are thirty-five or forty, you will have formed some impression of how death occurs and what are the circumstances you would want—or not want—to have when you are dying. If you're like most Americans, you will want to die with people around you. You will want to die relatively pain-free. You will want to have sufficient funds to support your care. You will want to retain as much control as possible over your care. You will want spiritual and emotional comfort. You will want to be at home.

So as you begin this internal dialogue anew—or for the first time—focus on these issues. Read about long-term care. Read about palliative care (in this book and elsewhere). Talk to people who have relatives in nursing homes, in hospices, at home. Put your thoughts down on paper if it makes it easier for you.

From these readings and this research will come some sort of internal ordering of your priorities and values. You'll establish a sense of how you would want to be treated or how you would want to see others in your family treated if and when they become seriously ill. (And keep in mind, we're not necessarily talking about when you're dying. Chronic illnesses also require this kind of thinking.)

The Conversation

After your internal monologue—sorting out what you consider quality of life—or even while you're doing that sorting, you're going to want to convey to someone you care about, or whose advice you trust, your feelings and thoughts and plans. This may be a spouse, a parent, a child, a physician, a spiritual adviser, or a lawyer. It should be someone who can influence your care or make decisions for you and your family, someone who can keep those who don't know your plans from disrupting them.

The very fact that you have communicated something about your thoughts and wishes to someone else means that you have taken an important step toward protecting yourself from loneliness, pain, and loss of control.

To do this right, you will want to have more than a single conversation about death and dying. It needs to be more of an ongoing dialogue that begins with one discussion and repeats itself from time to time, perhaps even up to the moment you die.

It's not hard to start such a conversation. Most people welcome it if they're ill. For instance, if you have a close friend who's seriously ill, you might ask, "What are your plans when you can't get around anymore?" Or ask whether they've heard of palliative care or hospice. Get a feel for what other people are doing and what they're comfortable with.

Eventually you will want to put your thoughts on paper, but the conversations themselves provide others with a guide to how *you* are thinking. You may say, "I want to have the most advanced pain medication," or "I want to die at home, surrounded by my family," or "I want to be in a hospital and kept alive even when I'm no longer conscious." These kinds of statements are the basis for a plan for your dying days, something that someone else can follow if you no longer can give instructions. The conversation is not just a means of telling someone about your wishes. It can also be a very valuable way of helping you to be more clear about them. In these conversations, you will find out whether you are making yourself absolutely clear, whether you have thought things through, whether there are areas of confusion. You will get important feedback that may help you make your ideas about these matters much more specific. For instance, what do you mean by "kept alive" when you're no longer conscious? For how long? Or what do you mean by "pain medication?" Does that include medicine that might put you into a sleep so deep that you can't communicate with loved ones?

The questions may seem simplistic, but most people find that when they get into talking about these matters, little details get in the way. And it is often in the details that the distinction between comfort and discomfort lies.

These are just some of the ideas you want to articulate before it begins "raining," though you will undoubtedly change some of the plans and ideas when you become ill.

Advance Directives

My advance directive allows me to say what I want to happen: if I am close to death and life support would only postpone the moment of death, I want no life support. If life support would not help my medical condition and would make me suffer permanent and severe pain, I do not want feeding tubes. I authorize my health care agent to direct my health care when I cannot do so.

—Geraldine R., dying of breast cancer

As we explained above, *advance directives* is a term that encompasses two main types of documents: the living will and the medical power of attorney, plus variations on that theme, such as Five Wishes, a document that incorporates all the themes we're talking about in this book. None of these documents require a lawyer, though each state has variations on them. They do require witnesses. Last Acts Partnership's Web site (www.lastactspartnership.org) will allow you to download and print your own state's particular set of advance directives and give you clear instructions about completing them.

The *living will* tells the world what you want at the end of your life if you can't speak for yourself. It says, "If I'm in a terminal condition and I can't communicate, this piece of paper speaks for me about the kind of treatment I do or do not want."

Do you want feeding tubes? Do you want to be on a breathing apparatus? Do you want antibiotics for pneumonia if you're already dying of cancer? If your quality of life wouldn't be significantly improved, how much pain medication do you want?

The living will form gives you room to put down what you do and do not want, but that's a little tricky. How much detail should you put in? What if you change your mind? What if you don't know what may be available five, ten, fifteen years from now? What if you're not specific enough? (Physicians and others point out that "no advanced life support" is too vague to offer real guidance.) What if you're *too* specific?

Physicians say the answer is to talk about these issues with them, to have a conversation that says, "Is this true under all circumstances, or only specific circumstances?" Sadly, there are many factors that get in the way of such conversations when you need them (see below.)

So there is another advance directive that can make the living will less ambiguous. The *medical power of attorney* (sometimes called a power of attorney for healthcare) gives the power to make *all* decisions about your health care to someone you choose to act for you (called the agent or proxy), but *not just when you're in a terminal condition*. This power of attorney for your health care is valid *any* time you can't act or communicate for yourself. For instance, if you're having an operation and are out of communication with your physicians, an agent can address issues that might arise. If you are in a coma, an agent can make decisions according to what you've said you want, or in your best interest. If you are nearing the end of life as a result of a worsening illness, such as ALS, a disease that reduces your ability to move and communicate, your agent can make the kinds of decisions you would have made if you could speak. The agent you choose might be a husband, a daughter, a cousin, or a good friend.

But—and this is crucial—the living will and proxy work well only if you and your family and agent have those conversations we wrote about above. All the issues surrounding serious illnesses and death need to be considered. Talking together gets issues out on the table, and allows the agent to know what you want. It also allows your family members to have their say and to understand everything involved. Remember, though, that this needs to be a conversation that is occasionally reviewed over a period of time—hopefully well before any medical emergency.

The bad news? Despite requirements that health care providers tell patients about advance directives, in 2002 only 15 to 20 percent of the general population had written them.

Changing Ideas about Advance Directives

For a number of years, discussions about advance directives focused on living wills. It was thought that this would enable you to achieve the kind of death that you wanted. Research, however, uncovered the fact that many such pieces of paper were not written with enough specificity to do so. Others had too much detail and were just as useless, tying the hands of medical personnel.

More recently, a power-of-attorney appointing a health-care agent has become the instrument that people felt would solve end-of-life problems. Having someone who could speak for you under any serious circumstances should have solved the issue. But this, too, works only under some circumstances. What if the agent isn't around when you go to the hospital? What if the agent and the family disagree on issues? What if the agent secretly disagrees with your choices?

Now there is more uniform agreement that a series of conversations you will have with your agent and your family over a number of years can provide the basis for a good relationship with your agent, between agent and family, and between your family and you; and better ensure that your wishes are understood, agreed upon, and made clear to your health care team.

Communicating with Health Care Professionals

None of this will work if you don't also communicate with your health care professionals—your internist and specialists—about your wishes. In fact, the very purpose of advance directives, and of having ideas about what you want done when you have a life-threatening illness, is to be able to communicate wishes to physicians and other professionals.

In chapters 2 and 3, we talked about how the system can be an obstacle to getting good end-of-life care. We talked about how physicians often join with us in a conspiracy of silence about death and dying. Let's look at the issue again.

The idea that a dialogue is the desired event between a doctor and a patient is not an old and hallowed one. Many of us grew up believing that our job was to present ourselves to a doctor and that he or she would then cure us. Many physicians, especially in these days of managed care, do not have the time for a dialogue. They want to get in there and get the job done.

But when we are beyond the stage of a broken arm or a rash on our stomach, when truly serious diseases are being considered, we need more than a nod and a cast or ointment. We need a truly deep and complete conversation.

Conclusions from one Department of Health and Human Services study make the point very well.

- According to patients who are dying and their families who survive them, lack of communication with physicians and other health care providers causes confusion about medical treatments, conditions, and prognoses, and the choices that patients and their families need to make. One study indicated that about one-third of patients would discuss advance care planning if the physician brought up the subject, while about one-fourth of patients are under the impression that advance care planning is only for people who were very ill or very old. Only 5 percent of patients stated that they found discussions about advance care planning too difficult.
- Studies have shown that discussing advance care planning and directives with a doctor increased patient satisfaction among patients age sixty-five years and over.
- Compared to agents of patients who *did not* have a living will, agents of patients with a living will who had discussed its content with the patient reported greater understanding, better confidence in their ability to predict the patient's preferences, and a stronger belief in the importance of having advance directives.
- Finally, patients who had advance discussions with their physicians continued to discuss and talk about these concerns with their families. Such discussions could enable patients and families to reconcile their differences about end-of-life care and help the family and physician come to agreement if they should need to make decisions for the patient.

Communication Breakdown

You may, with the best intentions, not broach the subject with your doctor until you have been told that you have a serious, perhaps life-threatening illness such as cancer. At that point, it may be difficult to even get out the most important questions: "How serious is this?" "Can you cure it?" The "wrong" answer to that question could give you news that you don't want to hear, news that could shake you to your foundations. And look at it from the point of view of the physician who has given you that news. He or she trained to be a healer, not the giver of bad news. He or she would much rather tell you that there is a miracle cure for your illness, or that it is a very minor case, or anything but that it is a life-threatening condition for which the doctor has no miracles at hand.

So what happens? Two people reluctant to use the simplest words—words that could spell unpleasantness for both of them—often fall back on terms or ideas that mask the seriousness of the situation. The physician may use jargon. The patient may fall back on silence or bafflement.

Lukas's Story

When Lukas was first diagnosed with lymphoma, the physician told him not to worry: this was not an acute disease, but rather a chronic one.

To the physician the word *chronic* was meant to convey that Lukas would live a long time, and that if the cancer recurred, it could be dealt with, even that Lukas would probably die of some other ailment before this particular cancer could kill him.

To Lukas, the word *chronic* was a death knell; it meant he was saddled with a permanent disease that would change his life and lifestyle forever. He might even be crippled by it.

Neither doctor nor patient realized that the other was misunderstanding the meaning each took from this word. It would be another two months before the matter was straightened out. Such is the power of fear when cancer is involved.

This is not the end of the difficulty. Sometimes, perhaps because of managed care and its curtailment of time in a doctor's office, perhaps because of the temperament of your doctors, you don't get to express your feelings and needs.

Ethnic or cultural differences also can get in the way. The gap between common parlance and medical jargon is more like a canyon. Here's what Gwendolyn London, D.Min., interim director of the Duke Institute on Care at the End of Life, Duke Divinity School, has to say about this issue:

> Those of us who work in this field understand all the jargon. We have the trigger words. We know what hospice is, we know what palliative care is. We know what advance directives are. We know advance care planning. We know all of that. But what we don't know is that the average person walking down the street, or walking in through the door of a hospital, or coming to visit a relative in an intensive care unit does not have the same understanding of those words. And as a matter of fact I know in the African-American community some of those words are very off-putting. So, not only do you have the problem with the language and the meanings not being shared, but you also have the additional problem of the words that are accepted and used universally by the health care professional being words that have negative connotations.

Trust is key to communication between patient and medical team. Unfortunately, there are disparities between the nature of care given to "mainstream" Americans and those from other cultures. Recent newspaper accounts report that African Americans receive less adequate care for the same ailments than do white Americans. And several years back a study reported that "Hispanics seen for fractures in a Los Angeles emergency room were twice as likely as non-Hispanic whites to be *under-treated* for pain."

But we're not talking just about cultural differences.

You may actually fear that if you do speak up and say you don't think you're getting the treatment you want, then you won't get *any* treatment; that if you say, well, this isn't the way you want to do things, the health care system will say, then take your needs elsewhere. In fact, this is against any code of ethics for health care, and it almost never happens. But you may fear it will.

Painful issues are hard to discuss. Conversations with physicians are often hindered, too, by our inability to raise emotionally difficult subjects. Some research we read says that women, more than men, fear death, or at least fear the process of dying. Perhaps that is so, but we suspect that it's also possible that in this—as in so many respects—men are less likely to talk about their feelings than are women. Which means, perhaps, that men are more likely than women to be hiding feelings that should be out in the open. And, whether male or female, young or old, feelings that remain buried are likely to interfere with your ability to cope with the threat that someday it will be time to die.

The result of all these missteps in communication can be crucial in your care.

In a paper published by the Radio and Television New Directors Association ("Covering the Issues of Death and Dying: A Journalist's Resource Guide," Washington, D.C., 1998) the authors had this to say about some of the choices that physicians make on your behalf: "Physicians write more DNR orders for people 75 or older than for those younger than 75, regardless of patients' preferences or prognoses, according to an August 14, 1996, article published in *The Annals of Internal Medicine.*"

So, yes, communicating with health care professionals is difficult. Which is precisely why discussions must take place between all members of the family, the health care team, and others until you feel confident you are getting and will keep getting just what you want.

It is also why you need to have both written instructions that can be referred to when necessary *and* a health care agent.

Improving Communications with Your Health Care Team

We've stressed communication as a key element of good end-of-life care, in fact, of all care. It is something that can be learned. Here are some thoughts.

The Preliminaries

1. First of all, make sure that you know what you want to ask, or to communicate to, your doctor.
2. Try to talk about end-of-life issues before a health care crisis comes up. It'll be much easier to do this if you're having just a regular yearly checkup, or going to the doctor for some routine matter.
3. Most physicians these days will welcome such a discussion. It's not important that you cover all the bases, just that you and the doctor

know that a series of questions exist and that you—and she—have some ideas about the answers. The doctor may take this opportunity to reassure you that she is associated with a hospital where full-scale palliative care is in practice. At the least, you will have instilled in the doctor the knowledge that you have thoughts about end-of-life care. And at the least, the doctor should ask you to send her a copy of your advance directives to go into your file.

Later On

The time may come, of course, when you are going in for a checkup for something that you think may be serious. You may be frightened. You may not have thought about end-of-life issues for some time, and right now, all you want to know is whether you have a serious problem. So:

- Write down the issues that are bothering you.
- If you're worried that you might not be able to ask all the right questions, bring someone along. Jamie Von Roenn, an oncologist in Chicago, recommends that as a common practice. Someone has to be able to listen, take notes, and remember what was said. It can prove very reassuring later, or at least provide material for getting a second opinion. Later, in the calm of your living room, the two of you can compare notes.
- Every good meeting with a patient should begin with the patient stating in whatever terms he or she wishes what is bothering him or her that day, and what the patient needs from the physician.
- When you're with a doctor who may be giving you bad news, try to listen without leaping ahead. It may take the doctor a long time to get to the diagnosis; it may even be that he has to send you for a lot of tests. Don't jump ahead in your mind. There is always time to panic. And if it occurs to you, remind the doctor that you do (or don't) have advance directives.
- Ask for a translation. It's not unusual for physicians to use medical jargon to explain a diagnosis or to describe your medical needs. If you don't understand what they're saying, get them to say it in plain English.
- Next, there are the days and weeks following a diagnosis. Doctors often tell us that they want to hear from their patients, that they are willing to take phone calls as a follow-up to the personal visit. This may not always

be easy. Well-meaning nurses or secretaries may try to shield the physician from a phone call. You may have to wait on hold or for a few days to receive a call back. Be persistent. You have the right to clarify everything about your diagnosis and potential treatments.

- If your disease turns out not to be curable, but is not immediately life-threatening, you need to be able to communicate to your physician exactly the kind of care you want, when you want to have cutting-edge treatment and when you have had enough. And, certainly, that goes for later on, when a life-threatening illness or disease has taken away all hope of cure and death is more imminent.

- Finally, make sure you take (or send) your advance directives to your physicians' office(s). And always, always take them with you to the hospital if you're going in for an operation or other treatment.

What happens when you haven't thought ahead, when you haven't discussed these issues with your family, when you have no living will, no health care agent?

What follows may scare some readers, but that's not why we're including it. What we want to show is that this kind of iffiness can be totally avoided. All you have to do is follow the precepts in this chapter!

The Abril Family

When Rafael Abril knew that his father was going to have a bypass operation, he, his three siblings, and his mother met and talked. They knew about living wills, but they hadn't made one up for themselves or for Mr. Abril.

Shortly after the bypass, Mr. Abril had a stroke. It became abundantly clear that he would not survive for long. The hospital called the family together and asked whether Mr. Abril should be kept on life support.

"We wished we'd decided before," Ms. Abril confided to us, her lined face clearly distraught. "It's up to us and we don't know what to do." It was not only that they didn't know what to do, but that this was the worst time in the world to be making such decisions. A physician at the hospital asked the family to step into a conference room. He told them that there would be a series of decisions to be made. Should machines be used to continue to breathe for Mr. Abril if he went into cardiac arrest? Should they cut a tracheotomy if need be? What medications should be used? How long should they persist?

"If only we'd asked him before," Ms. Abril said as she held the hand of a priest in the hallway.

The night wore on without decisions being made. The spiritual comfort offered by the priest was not enough to help this large family that had made no preparation for this painful moment.

Finally, in the early hours, the Abrils decided to let their father go off the ventilator—to die. But even then, their worries continued. Had they done the right thing? Is it what he would have wanted? Since Mr. Abril had never told them—and they'd never asked—they never knew.

But this isn't going to happen to you.

No matter when you read this book, no matter at what point you come to it—before an illness or in its midst—you can make your choices about what to put in your living will. You can choose a health care agent and tell him or her what you want as the illness does or does not progress.

It's never too late.

7

Choosing an Agent

This may well be the most important chapter in this book. It will speak, in very direct terms, about how to choose a health care agent, and why it's important to do so. It will make clear the nuances, and spell out where this is simple and where it's a difficult set of tasks. This is not a theoretical matter: people throughout the country are finding that having the right health care agent (sometimes called *proxy* or *surrogate*) can be not only a necessary choice, but one that can relieve you from unnecessary care and worry for years to come. We will repeat some material here that was in the last chapter, but it is so important that it is worth saying over again.

The trouble with living wills bears repeating: experts once thought that putting careful thought into a living will would do the trick. On the day when you needed to have your wishes about the end of life known and adhered to, when accident or illness rendered you unable to communicate and in a state from which recovery was impossible, your hospital or nursing home would read your living will and follow its instructions.

But living wills are limited. If they're too specific, they tie doctors' hands; if you make them too general or too ambiguous, you hurt your cause. Some years ago, The Robert Wood Johnson Foundation produced a two-year study showing that in more than 75 percent of the cases, hospitals simply ignored patients' and families' wishes about resuscitation and other end-of-life decisions, even though a living will existed. Why? Because the will may leave out things that you didn't know about when you were writing it, or may make requests that aren't clear to a hospital, or, worse yet, you've changed your mind, but didn't write a new living will. They're open to interpretation or they may be ignored because they don't seem to reflect your best interests.

So what if a hospital or physician chooses not to follow your wishes, even if they know about your living will? What if the staff is so busy trying to keep you alive they can't—or won't—pay attention? What if there are disputes in your family over how you should be cared for? What then?

The answer is to have one person who will fight for you—to make sure *your* wishes are honored—and that is what this and the next chapter are about. That person is your agent.

The agent is a person whom you absolutely trust to carry out what *you* wish, someone who will put aside his or her preferences and values to honor yours. It is someone who will be there when you need him to be, who will educate himself about your health care and your particular needs. It may or may not be a family member, and family members may or may not be upset that you choose someone else. Never mind. The goal is to have a person in control if you can no longer be; who acts for you as you would act if you could.

In most states, your physician is prohibited from being your agent; so are nurses or the staff of a nursing home. The reasons for this are straightforward: conflict of interest. Even though doctors are becoming more and more educated and interested in alternatives when cure is no longer an option, their primary job is to look to your cure. An agent's job is to look to your wishes, whatever they may be. When the time comes—and this is important—your agent will need to consult with physicians, clergy, social workers, and family members about your care, but in the end, the decision should be the agent's, acting as he or she believes you would want.

For the time being, this is all abstract, but we hope to make it crystal-clear by including in this chapter some excerpts from conversations between actual agents and "principals" (a term meaning the person for whom the agent is acting—*you*.)

In this chapter we will concentrate on the agent–principal partnership, and on how your wishes can be known and carried out by that agent. This relationship is legally recognized by every state in the United States. In other words, the agent–principal relationship is a legally binding and powerful one. Hospitals, physicians, nursing homes, hospices, and next of kin must all acknowledge it. This will go a long way toward helping you get what you want, and will allow your agent to respond to your changing medical circumstances and help make sure that your wishes are carried out. In the next chapter, we discuss how your agent can go about doing this most efficaciously.

Qualifications

Choosing someone who will vigorously advocate for you is one of the most important decisions you will ever make—the most powerful step to retaining control over the end of your life. What kind of person should this be?

- First, a simple but important qualification: if at all possible, you should pick someone who lives near enough so that he or she will be able to come to your side when the time comes, without undue effort. In short, you want your agent available.
- Pick someone who will be willing to sit down with you and discuss your wishes, to really listen.
- Pick someone who understands you, who is *simpatico*.
- Pick someone who is not so young that she cannot comprehend your need to let go when the time comes (if that is your choice), but someone not so old or ill that she may become incapacitated before you. We often want to pick someone who is our own age or even older. But if you're contemplating a nice long life, do you want someone as agent who might die before you? Or someone whose physical and mental stamina might be diminished when you most need them? Maybe a younger person would serve you better.
- Pick someone with a great deal of gumption. You are asking this person to see you through a very difficult time under very trying circumstances.
- Pick someone who will follow your wishes no matter how she may feel, but pick someone who can also think independently, who is willing to get help from experts if there is a conflict about your wishes or a decision to be made that neither of you had contemplated (for instance, new medical advances that your agent is called upon to think about and that you and she could not possibly have discussed or anticipated).
- And always keep in mind that your wishes will change over time. It happens to all of us as our values change, as we have families and grandchildren, as we get a chronic disease that we didn't think we could bear but discover we can live with. So pick someone as an agent who can be as flexible as you.

That's a lot of qualifications, but millions of people are finding that they can pick someone who can, in fact, decide in their best interests.

The Usual Suspects

Let's look at a few likely candidates and discuss things to keep in mind as you consider which would make the best agent for you.

A Family Member

Sometimes the best person to choose as an agent is a close family member. In fact, most people do choose a spouse or adult child. They feel that a family member knows them best. Or they feel that a family member may have more legal or moral clout in these matters when it comes to making a crucial choice at a time of crisis. Or they worry about offending a spouse if they choose someone outside the family. So if you feel strongly that it *should* be a close relative who will vigorously advocate for you, that's fine.

A Close Friend

On the other hand, it may turn out that a friend is more willing to contemplate the matter of your death without feeling frightened by it than a husband or sister, someone who may be too invested in keeping you around, no matter what transpires. (Of course, the reverse can be true, too. A friend may fear losing her best pal, or may not have the perseverance of a family member.) Even the most intelligent and loving relative who has sworn to abide by your wishes may feel pressure from other family members or from his or her own conscience or fear of loss to act in your best interest.

How We Made Our Decisions

We think it might be helpful to tell you how we made these decisions.

Kaplan: There are several reasons why I want my son to be my agent. For one thing, we've had a chance to talk about my wishes several times. Not as dinner table conversation, but, over the years, on and off, especially since my mother's death. He understands what I want, and I feel that he'll know how to handle matters if the going gets tough. But there's another reason: I don't know when or where I might need him to deal with decisions about my death. If it's in some hospital in another state or where they have negative feelings about removing life support, a member of my immediate family just may have more authority than a friend or distant relative. I don't want *anything* getting in the way of my achieving the goals in my living will.

Lukas: On some level, I would prefer not to have my wife make the decision to withdraw my life support, or to prevent it from being used in the first place. As often as we have discussed these matters, a part of me feels that it's not fair. How can she be asked to let me go after all these years of marriage? Why should I burden her with that kind of decision? She has made it clear to me, by the way, that my love for her and my wish to keep her around might stand in the way of my adhering to *her* wishes. So while my wife is in fact my agent, she has chosen one of our daughters to be *her* agent. Lingering doubts remain. Perhaps they always will. We have talked about alternative proxy choices, but so far have done nothing about changing our present ones.

Just describing the requirements for an agent doesn't do justice to the nuances. So we've chosen—from many possibilities—a real-life story that illustrates why having the right agent is crucial, and how different circumstances demand different skills.

Emil

At the age of sixty-five, Emil knew that his heart would someday give out, because he had had several minor heart attacks and a bypass operation, and plaque continued to build up in his arteries; he was one of those people for whom heart disease was persistent. On the other hand, he had survived so far, and he was still not an old man, and he didn't want someone to assess treating him as "futile," to abandon resuscitation efforts should "the big one" come. Because he had recently signed on with a managed care insurance company, Emil was also fearful that saving money might play a role in his caretakers' decisions not to keep him alive.

He did not entirely trust his children to be able to deal with the matter when the moment came. So he discussed his wishes with his niece, Agnes, who agreed to see him through whatever happened. The two of them sat down several times and, over the years, came to an agreement as to various routes of action that should be taken under different circumstances.

And the moment *did* come. Emil was stricken on the street, near his home. The EMS ambulance rushed him to a nearby hospital, where no one knew his wishes. Agnes was alerted because her uncle carried a card with her number in his wallet. She arrived at the hospital to discover Emil going into cardiac arrest. A Code Blue was called, and physicians began to use all the tools at their disposal—from electric stimulation to drugs—to keep Emil alive. Soon he was stabilized. But overnight in the ICU, an infection occurred, and Agnes was informed that her uncle was in terminal condition. One young physician made an appeal to the team to give up the "futile" effort. Agnes demurred, insisting that more efforts be pursued. The physician asked to see some proof that she represented Emil's wishes. By this time his two daughters and son had arrived at the hospital, and they, as foreseen by Emil, were unable to help in the decisionmaking. Agnes had the proxy papers, and with the evidence that she was legally in charge, Emil received every last effort. He was brought back from the brink and actually lived two more years.

The assets of having a strong and savvy agent should be evident by now. We hope we've made equally plain the necessity of choosing wisely and communicating your wishes to that person with clarity. If you do so, you have a much better chance of having your wishes preserved up to the very end.

Talking with Your Agent

Whichever choice you make, it's crucially important to delve into your agent's feelings. Does she understand your wishes? If not, just how different are her own feelings? Different enough to stand in the way of handling your death the way you want it handled? And how tough-minded is he? Can your husband deal with your dying wishes while undergoing the grief of losing you? Can any of your adult children do the same? Can an aunt or a niece? If not, who can? Only you can be the judge of how your own son or daughter, niece, or nephew might act, and your relative should be ready to admit his or her doubts and fears to you before signing on as your agent. Talking—and listening—will help you make that judgment.

The conversations we've been talking about are not just about choosing an agent; they are meant to inform the agent, as precisely as you can, about your values, your wishes, and your needs when it comes to quality of life during a serious illness and treatment for that illness. Any detail, every change of mind, every doubt should be communicated to your agent. The thing you don't want to happen is that you have some idea about your care—based on emotion or knowledge acquired since your last conversation—and because of a sudden accident or ailment, you never get to tell your agent about your thoughts. If the agent is the right person for you, both of you will feel good about these ongoing conversations.

Assume now that you have chosen someone: your daughter or a close friend—someone you've known for a number of years. She agrees to consider serving as your agent. Before making your actual decision, you will want to sit down with her, perhaps several times over the course of several years, to talk about what you have in mind. The same questions you asked yourself when you thought about values, when you wrote a living will or first spoke with your family, should be raised and thought through one more time:

- What scares me about dying?
- Where do I want to die?
- What kind of medical treatment do I want? (This is actually a dozen or more questions—but we'll get to that.)
- Who do I want around me?
- What kind of spiritual counseling or comfort do I want? When?
- How do I want my family to remember me?
- What do I want to complete in my life before I become incapacitated?
- Do my partner, my children, my doctor know what's important to me?

Those are big questions, so don't expect to have ready answers to them at a first sitting. In fact, the conversations themselves provide others with a guide to how you are thinking. You may say, "I want to have the most advanced pain medication" or "I want to die at home, surrounded by my family" or "I want to be in a hospital and kept alive even when I'm no longer conscious." These kinds of statements are the basis for a plan for your dying days, something that someone else can follow when you no longer can give instructions. But these conversations are not just a means of telling someone about your wishes. They can also be a very valuable way of helping you clarify your own ideas. The best agents will be quick to let you know if you are making yourself absolutely clear, will prompt you to revisit some things to think them through again, and will point out contradictory or confusing directives. As we suggested in an earlier chapter, you will get important feedback that may help you make your ideas about these matters much more specific.

Most people find that when they get into talking about these matters, little details get in the way. And it is often in the details that the distinction between comfort and discomfort lies.

These are ideas you want to articulate before it begins raining, although you will undoubtedly change some of the plans and ideas when you become ill, as you experience what you can and cannot bear to think about or to undergo.

"Putting a Toe in the Water": Beginning a Conversation

How do you actually go about beginning such a conversation? Isn't that difficult? Luckily, others have led the way. First, some general thoughts.

Lots of people have difficulty imagining how to begin conversations about dying. The result is that they often wait until someone else—a doctor, a son, a niece—brings up the issues. That's fine. It doesn't have to be the principal (you) who begins. It can be the potential agent; it can be a friend; it can be a son or daughter. Of course, even then, it's often hard, which is why we suggested that the first thing is simply to think about the issues. Read about them. Think back on situations you've known about where you thought the end-of-life care and circumstances were right, and ones where they were wrong.

Then if, say, you have a parent who isn't talking about these matters, you might refer to a recent death and say how you felt about it.

If you want to tell your feelings to your daughter or husband, you might do the same thing. Don't be surprised if someone says to you, "Oh, I don't want to talk about such things," or "That's a gruesome thing to bring up."

You can get past that by dropping the subject for now; or if you feel it's important to talk at this time, you can say, "Well, it's something I've been thinking about. I'd like to get it off my chest."

But you know your family or friends better than we. You'll figure out how to bring it up, because it will be in your best interest to do so, and we should always be able to find a way of bringing up things that are in our best interest.

Mother and Daughter

Here's one such actual story. A mother had already chosen her husband as her agent, but she was now considering asking her eldest daughter (a budding physician) to do the job instead. She worried, for instance, that if the moment came when she would want to be allowed to die peacefully, without attempts to constantly resuscitate her, her husband might not be able to let her go.

So one day in late spring, she sits down to discuss with her daughter what she would want if she were seriously ill. While the mother comes into this discussion having talked about it with her husband and having thought she knew what she wanted, she finds the conversation extremely helpful in perfecting the nuances. And at the end, the daughter comes away with a clear mandate to do certain things for her mother when she is stricken.

The mother starts by saying, "I guess there are a bunch of scenarios that could happen. Let's talk about the car accident scenario."

Right away, the mother has set the stage for a specific kind of end-of-life possibility: the sudden accident, rather than the lingering chronic illness. In this case, she would be rushed to the hospital and a trauma team would be summoned. What would she want her daughter to do? "I would want to be kept alive if there was any chance that I could recover and have life with quality." The key word, of course, is quality.

The daughter thinks about this, then says, "What if they said there's a twenty percent chance, but you'll have to be on a ventilator for the next six months?" The ventilator—a breathing apparatus—might be needed because of damage to the nerves preventing the mother from breathing for herself, but the hidden question here is: What if she *never* recovers the ability to breathe by herself? Does she want to be on a ventilator forever?

The mother responds this way: "If at the end of the six months, they thought I could lead a normal life, I would want you to do that. I would want you to keep me alive unless it became clear to you that I couldn't have a meaningful life. By meaningful I mean that I would be able to relate to other people. I could be in a wheelchair, that would be okay."

"In other words," says the daughter, "you'd be okay if it was only physical damage, but what about mental capacity?"

The mother says, "What's important to me is the ability to relate to people and to recognize people. And to be who I am. Because I don't think that my physical abilities define who I am. But my mental capacities and my relating capacities do."

Note how specific the mother is about what concerns her. Note how the daughter keeps probing to find the nuances. None of this was planned; no one had taught the two of them how to communicate about this. Still, it flows naturally between them, because they honestly want to get it right.

Next the daughter asks about pain in the context of a different scenario—one in which her mother's decline is longer-term.

The mother says, "If I had terminal cancer and we were past the point of surgery and chemotherapy, then hospice is what appeals to me. I'd like to be kept as physically comfortable as I could be. And I know that's doable. Pain management is good. And I'd like my family to be there as much as possible. And then I'd like to be allowed to die peacefully. Do you think you could do that?"

This is a somber moment. All of a sudden the theoretical slips aside, and it is painfully real in the room. The daughter nods, slowly, three times. Then: "I think Daddy might be less able to emotionally disconnect from the situation and look at really what you would want, as opposed to how he would be feeling about the situation, but I think that even though I would be obviously distraught if anything terrible happened to you, and I had to watch you suffer, or watch you be sick, I think that I could look at what you would want, and respect that. Even though I might not make that choice myself."

The conversation ends with the mother saying, "Yes, I'm comfortable that you would do what you felt I would want you to do."

What a wonderful conversation. What a relief it must have been for the two of them.

Husband and Wife

Because these kinds of conversations can be instructive, here's another one for you to think about as a guide to having your own.

Henry and Kathy Chalfant had been married almost thirty years when they finally sat down and had "the discussion." Each agreed to be the agent for the other. But what did they want? With what circumstances would each be faced? And under what pressures would they have to act? Rather than do this in a general fashion, the Chalfants sat down under the guidance of Dr. Joseph J. Fins, chief of the Division of Medical Ethics at Weill Medical College of Cornell University. Fins and his team were already working on a project to help patients and proxies better understand their responsibilities to each other, particularly through having meaningful conversations. This educational project, called *Fidelity, Wisdom & Love,* includes the video of the Chalfants' discussion and a workbook that uses a set of common medical scenarios, from cancer to Alzheimer's, to promote very detailed and specific discussions about end-of-life decisionmaking, particularly within a hospital setting.

The workbook's scenarios ask their patient/proxy readers to consider such questions as whether to remove a breathing machine and under what circumstances. The answers then become the basis for further discussion, as we see in the video when Mr. and Mrs. Chalfant reconsider, reaffirm or discard previously thought-out decisions.

Key to the team's thinking is that what they call a *covenant* exists between proxy and patient—a bond, often based on previously close relationships—so that the decisionmaking is two-way. In other words, while the "patient" is telling the proxy what he or she wants under certain circumstances, the bond between the two produces a discussion in which each influences the other, and the feelings they have about each other plays a part in the outcome of these discussions.

Here are some of the things that came out of the Chalfants' discussion.

First, the couple laughingly reminded each other that they were still at the stage in their lives when they thought they were immortal, but that they really knew better. They knew that in order for things to "work" in the hospital, a person really needs to have chosen somebody as agent or proxy. They knew from experience how important having an agent could be. In fact,

Henry Chalfant had been present at the bedside of his father, who had no proxy, while his wife had been agent for three family members. Both of them could see the difference it made.

In the first scenario in the workbook, Kathy imagined that she had cancer. Chemotherapy had worked for a while, but now "You have become weaker, and it appears that chemotherapy is not working. You are now brought to the hospital with a life-threatening pneumonia—you are unconscious and are not able to tell the doctors what sort of treatment you want. You are put on a breathing machine. If you were the patient, would you want to be removed from the breathing machine?"

For Kathy, it was a "tricky question." Would she come off the ventilator or would she not? "Faced with it, I think—well, of course I want to be removed from the ventilator . . . on the other hand there is a moment when I say—but perhaps I could get better."

Finally, she admits that pneumonia "wouldn't be a bad way to go," and her husband agrees that taking her off the ventilator and letting her die "mercifully" would be something he could do.

Then, in the middle of the conversation about her wishes, Henry brings up the experience with his father. "There wasn't a proxy, but we all knew that he felt very strongly—that you shouldn't go to great measures to revive a person, you know, when there was very little hope of recovery. But he was attached to the ventilator—and there was no advance directive, and he would look at you imploringly—some of us would say he's saying, 'I want to live!'—and some of us would say he's saying, 'Let me out of this!'"

He then adds, turning again to his wife's case, "But at the end of your life it's just prolonging it, and it's painful, and seems to be a waste."

Suddenly, without warning, he begins to cry. "It's very emotional," he says. And his wife can only look on with empathy.

The situation changes. Dr. Fins gives Henry a situation: He has a heart problem that has been around for some years. Suddenly it gets worse, and he is admitted to the intensive care unit. "After careful evaluation the doctor believes you may have a lung infection in addition to your heart problem. The doctor is not certain whether you will live or die."

Henry says right away he'd want to be removed from the breathing apparatus; he would want to be allowed to die.

But Kathy, saying that she knows him very well, suggests that he often thinks "in apocalyptic terms" and that perhaps this lung problem is actually treatable. Maybe, just maybe, he's got more life in him yet. Henry thinks about it and agrees that maybe he's acted too quickly. Maybe he's not terminal, and he'd want his wife to keep him alive to see if antibiotics would work.

There are as many kinds of conversations as there are people having them. Some are brief, and happen while you're making dinner together or in the car. Some are scheduled meetings specifically set up to discuss the issues at length. Not all of them produce such clear-cut and actionable results as the two we've cited. But *all* such conversations are a beginning point to sort out how to operate when the time comes.

When you're talking with the person you have chosen, note his or her reactions. If the person is going to be really good at this, he or she will explore your reasoning. The agent may even try to argue with you, because the agent needs to understand what you want. This will be a good exercise for you, too, helping you hone or (where appropriate) change your wishes. You will want to describe some of the scenarios that could occur, to probe whether your agent can handle them. Then, perhaps, you may ask her to think it over. Only after you have both agreed that your agent's understanding is deep and her willingness complete should you sign over responsibility to act on your behalf.

Change

It's important to remember that goals may change many times between now and the time you're (a) first diagnosed with a serious illness or (b) progressing through that illness. Similarly, your ability to communicate with your agent may change.

If you don't feel that your agent is still serving your needs and your values, don't hesitate to change. This can be an awkward thing to do, but it's imperative. Don't forget that it is your interests that are at heart, not your agent's. The easiest thing to do, usually, is to be honest, but not harmful. Tell your agent that you feel he or she isn't comfortable with the responsibility, that you've been talking with X, and that he seems comfortable, so you are relieving your agent of what could be an onerous responsibility. It may in fact be a relief to your old agent that he or she is being replaced.

8

BEING AN AGENT

W e hope that you are already contemplating choosing an agent. Someday you may be asked to be one, a serious responsibility that you should fully understand before you commit to it.

Before You Commit

No matter how much these ideas and wishes are thought about, no matter how many conversations are held, no matter how many documents are signed, it can be difficult for agents to carry out some of the decisions that you two have made together. The main reasons are threefold.

First, not all decisions are cut and dried. A sudden stroke, or the discovery that your cancer has come back or metastasized, or any other emergency situation can place great strains on the health care team, family, and agent to make the "right" decision. Perhaps this is the time to say that often there is no right decision; there is only the best decision under the circumstances. As one principal said to her chosen agent after discussing many of these issues in detail, "It's an imperfect process. It can't be done one hundred percent." It is all the more important that the agent try to take in your values and wishes before this situation occurs, for it is those values and wishes that need to be honored. This allows you, the patient, to participate in treatment decisions if illness or emergency has rendered you unable to communicate.

But knowing what someone would want under changed and changing circumstances is just not that easy. What if my husband isn't eating? Is that because he's about to die, or because it's painful to swallow, or because he's in distress of some other sort? Should he be fed? Does that run counter to your husband's wishes? What if there's a 5 percent chance of coming through the illness; should he be kept on a breathing machine? Is this a terminal ailment, or a chronic disease with sharp turns in its course? Maybe my father (son, grandparent) will get better and live a long time. The point is, even under the best of circumstances, doubts arise: "Are we doing the right thing?" "Is this the best ethical choice?" "Aren't we hastening death by withholding care?"

A hospital ethics consultant or a member of the clergy may help you put these fears to rest, but then again, they may not. Later on in this chapter, we'll detail how one agent, Bernice, looked after her dying mother's interests. At the end of the process, she said, "I think I made the right decision. But that doesn't mean it was easy. It was very hard!" Alzheimer's disease, HIV/AIDS, off-and-on-again heart problems, cancer that's spreading, depression—a myriad of things can put you to the test. The more you've talked ahead of time and thought about different scenarios, the better off you are.

Second, institutions and/or professionals—even with the best of intentions— can sometimes interfere with freedom of choice. Here are some examples from which we've drawn some important lessons.

A few days after surgery a ninety-one-year-old woman in a nursing home whose living will clearly said no heroic measures was having trouble breathing. She was sent to a nearby hospital and put on a respirator. Her daughters, who had power of attorney in case she could not make medical decisions for herself, discovered that the nursing home had not sent the proper documents to the hospital. Armed with the documents, they asked the hospital to turn off the respirator and let their mother die. The doctors said they couldn't. When the woman finally died, five days later, after the hospital had finally been persuaded that it was legal and ethical to turn off the respirator, the daughters were still distraught. "It was five extra days of miserable life. We were feeling terribly guilty. We didn't do our job."

The Lesson: If someone enters a nursing home, special care has to be taken that the home is aware of advance directives and will let everyone else—especially other medical facilities—know about them. (Chapter 12 deals with nursing home issues in greater detail.)

A ninety-year-old man had advanced Alzheimer's disease. The son was named as agent. When the father came down with pneumonia, his son said *no* to treatment, because he knew it would only prolong his father's already painful, vegetative life. But a doctor insisted on giving him antibiotics. A counselor at Last Acts Partnership told the man's son to stick up for himself. "Don't let them bully you into anything."

The Lesson: It takes guts to be a good agent. You can't afford to alienate the hospital or nursing home, but you want to make sure you stay on top of things and do what you need to do to see your duties through to the proper course.

We interviewed Bernice some years ago. She had been the agent for her mother, whose progress from mild to severe dementia took many years, taking her from normal living at home, to assisted living in a facility, to nursing home care, to final days in a hospital. Throughout it all, Bernice kept uppermost in her mind what she knew her mother did and did not want. Bernice was fully committed to her role.

- She took her responsibility seriously. "You know, it seems to me that there are only two tasks in life: You bring kids up and bring them into the world and nurture them so they can go on, and you help the other generation get out with a minimum of difficulty. And I began to realize this was what I'm supposed to be doing now with my life."
- She made sure that she knew her mother's wishes. "She and my father would come home from visiting someone in a hospital, and they would say, oh, my God—why don't they just let them go?! Why are they keeping them alive?" Bernice made written notes of these conversations, establishing a concrete record of her mother's wishes.
- She made sure that she was well educated about her mother's particular condition, attending classes in dementia when she could, reading what she needed to read.
- She let the nursing home personnel know who she was, that she wasn't an expert in medical care, but that she *was* an expert in what her mother wanted. "And that's part of it. That's part of the job, you know—it's not just 'oh, sign this.'" In return, the nursing home responded by making her a true partner in the care of her mother, so there were few nasty surprises.

But there were bound to be some surprises, and the end of her mother's life was one such moment. Bernice was away for the weekend when her mother stopped eating and was discovered to have a urinary infection. A physician phoned Bernice and said that her mother needed antibiotics, but he didn't want to give them unless Bernice approved, because it said clearly in her mother's chart that all life-preserving methods, especially all "tubes," should be cleared with her. Because it seemed to be a temporary insertion of a tube, something designed not to artificially keep her mother alive, but to cure her temporary infection, Bernice approved it. But the veins in her mother's arms were collapsing, and an IV could not be inserted. Then the physician asked permission to give oxygen, since Bernice's mother was having trouble breathing. That, too, was okay with Bernice, but soon her mother died. And that's when Bernice said, "I did the right thing. But it was still hard!"

The Lesson: Institutions and professionals won't see it as their responsibility to carry out your loved one's wishes. They have many patients and in an emergency may not think about those wishes. *You* have to think of failsafes and put them into operation.

Often, agent and principal do not have the kind of communication between them that is necessary to make the relationship a complete and fruitful one.

Take this case: Marjorie was asked to be the agent for a man she'd known only a few months. When Marjorie responded, "But I don't know what you want or what your values are," the man said, "Oh, of course you do!" That was the end of the discussions between them. A copy of the man's medical power of attorney arrived in the mail. It took a few years before Marjorie had the courage to write him back and say, "I can't do this unless you do me the courtesy of discussing your needs and wishes with me. It just won't work." She never heard from him again about this issue.

At present, most health care agents seem to be women. That will change as more men learn that there is something extraordinarily rewarding about being an agent for a loved one or friend. On the other hand, the value of having a "mothering" kind of agent does not sound bad to the authors.

An Important Exercise

Put down on paper those qualities you want from an agent. Think carefully; it may affect your physical and mental well-being some day.

Then put down on paper those qualities you would want in your principal if you were *acting* as an agent. Think carefully: having responsibility for
someone you may dislike or who doesn't give you enough information can
be a burden. There should be something more than anxiety or hard work
about being an agent. To do it right requires both a sense of obligation and
a joy of giving.

Communication Is the Key

Agenting is not a matter of legal knowledge or of a contest between bull-
headed people. It's a matter of feeling what needs to be done and caring
enough to see that it's carried out.

Bernice showed us that complete communication with the medical team
is possible. The skills she employed—concern, but not interference; inquir-
ing, but not demanding; offering help, but not insisting—allowed her to
both inform and be kept informed of all that was going on.

We have talked several times about the "health care team," but until now
we have not fully defined it. If you are a patient or an agent or just an
onlooker, you will want to know just exactly who is on this team, of which
the patient is the heart.

Let's take the agent's point of view. Think ahead to the day when someone for whom you are serving as agent is in need of medical help, when he
or she has a serious illness. Your friend may or may not be "dying" at that
point—it depends partly on your perspective on that word, and partly on
how the medical community looks at things—but you certainly want things
to go as well as they can.

How Does This Team Help?

- First off, if you ask the right questions, they can be a great source of
  information.
- They can be a great source of comfort.
- They can help put things in perspective—for instance, pointing out
  that you often don't have to rush to make a decision under certain circumstances. Time is not your enemy when the patient is on a breathing

apparatus and is unconscious. You can put your decision on hold to get a second opinion, to consult with family members, or just to think things through in the calm of your own home.

As agent, you can help make this team pull together. You can convey information from one member of the team to another. And whether the patient is in for some massive treatments or just in a state of fear of "what if," you want to know who is going to participate in his or her care and who you can count on to help weather the storm. So, who are these people?

Primary Care Physician

The primary care physician, of course, will, we hope, have discussed the "what ifs" of dying with the patient long ago, and have copies of the living will and the health care proxy.

Specialists

Whether this is a neurologist or oncologist or gastroenterologist, these are the specially trained doctors who are responsible for diagnosing and treating disease. Remember, we could be talking about cancer, we could be talking about ALS (Lou Gehrig's disease), we could be talking about a pneumonia or emphysema that has gotten out of control. Any and all of these will require at least one specialist. It pays to discuss your patient's wishes about end-of-life care with all of them. Do not assume that in their discussions with one another those items have been on the agenda.

Nurses

One thing we know for sure: often you will have more opportunity to talk with a skilled and congenial nurse than with the doctors. A nurse will take histories when patients arrive at the doctor's office. A nurse will find out what progress or lack of progress has been made. A nurse may be responsible for preparing the patient for treatment(s). More than that, the nurse usually has more time to sit and talk about needs and anxieties than does the doctor. And, often, many nurses have more empathy about these matters than do doctors, whose eyes are on treatment and cure rather than on personal feelings. To be fair, this is changing. For physicians, a mammoth nationwide education effort is under way under the direction of Dr. Linda Emanuel. Called *Educating Physicians about End of Life Care* (EPEC), it has the imprimatur of the American Medical Association. For nurses, it is ELNEC *(End of Life Nursing Education Consortium)*, under Betty Ferrell, R.N., Ph.D. Both have Web sites, which even laypeople may find fascinating because they show exactly what the medical world is doing to incorporate all the new wishes and demands of the patient, the agent, and others. Social workers and clergy are beginning to create their own educational organizations about end-of-life matters.

One final note about nurses: they come in all varieties. There are those who specialize in palliative care, those who are skilled in hospice work, and those whose primary responsibility is overseeing bedside care or home care. It's important to recognize some of these distinctions and for both patient and agent to communicate the right message to the right person.

Clergy

You may not want to seek help from members of the clergy. You or the patient or the patient's family may not be particularly religious or think a priest or rabbi can help. But they can deal with spiritual issues that are *not* religious, with questions of "Why now?" "Why me?" "What does suffering mean?"

The entire area of spiritual matters is dealt with in chapter 9, but for now, just keep in mind that clergy are there, in the care setting. And, more and more, clergy are learning to handle end-of-life matters better and better.

Social Workers

In some care settings, neither doctors nor nurses nor administrators have the time or know-how, or even desire, to calm the patient's fears or supply information. Often, a patient's tension and stress will not be relieved by any of them. But most institutions have social workers whose sole job is to help patients work through some of those issues. In many care settings, that service is free, or covered at least by part of the money that is being paid by an insurance company for treatment. A patient should be given that help. These social workers are people who are specially trained to help people who are facing death in their mind's eye. They have had experience with hundreds of similarly placed people. They can put a sense of abnormalcy into perspective. They can help separate your fears from reality.

Of course, anyone—patient or agent—is free to go to a counselor outside of health care settings, but the little secret worth knowing is that these social workers are already within the care setting, specifically to help with emotional and practical problems.

When patient or agent or family faces emotional stress, social workers and other counselors are there to help, and we hope no one—patient, agent, family member, or friend—will feel ashamed of going for psychological help. Make no mistake about it, being told you have a life-threatening illness is a trauma; being around someone who has a life-threatening illness is a trauma. Undergoing chemotherapy or radiation is disturbing. Wondering how long you have to live and how painful your illness will be is normal. Feeling stressed about it all is healthy. And acting *for* people undergoing those circumstances is equally upsetting. What's not healthy is to live with the stress and anxiety when there are specialists who can help relieve them.

A wonderful book on these matters is Dr. Roger Granet's *Surviving Cancer Emotionally.* It goes a long way toward helping understand the emotional stresses of physical illness and disease, and some of the ways to alleviate these emotional pains.

Others

There are others whose job it is to help you under these circumstances, and upon whom your agent can call.

There is the hospital department of patient representatives, whose job it is to make sure the hospital is treating you well, and that you're getting what you need.

And there are always the formal and informal caregivers, volunteers from hospice and family members who do the enormous job of looking after loved ones day after day after day (for more on this heroic work, see chapter 10).

Someone has suggested that the best way to think about being an agent is to think about what you would want from the person you might choose as an agent for yourself. Put yourself in the shoes of someone who wants to have the best decisions made in the best possible way under the worst circumstances. Who would you choose to do that for you? That's the kind of agent you should be if you agree to do it for someone else.

When Things Go Awry

The following is taken from a book by Daniel R. Tobin, M.D., *Peaceful Dying*. Tobin is the founder and director of The Life Institute, VA Health-Care Network Upstate New York at Albany, and an adjunct assistant professor in psychiatry at Dartmouth Medical School. It is a cautionary tale that is worth listening to.

When I was a medical intern, I worked at a large hospital as a house officer in charge of the intensive care and coronary care units for six consecutive weeks, working alternate twenty-four-hour shifts of one full day on, one day off, the next day on again, and so forth. On my twenty-fifth consecutive alternate day, a ninety-two-year-old woman was admitted for heart failure. Mrs. Rogers came into the hospital unconscious, curled up in the fetal position, her breathing shallow and labored.

On her chart were her advance directives, in which she clearly stated that no attempts should be made to resuscitate her and that she was to undergo absolutely no life-prolonging techniques in the face of irreversible disease.

By her hospital bedside were her two daughters, upset and anxious. Next to them, apparently much calmer, was Mrs. Rogers's granddaughter, a nurse at a local teaching hospital. Exhausted after too many nights in the coronary care unit, and assuming that I had a professional ally I could talk frankly with about the patient's advance directives, I asked the young woman what she thought of her grandmother's condition.

Suddenly, her expression changed. "We want to do everything for Grandma, everything possible!" she said passionately.

Caught completely off guard by her sudden release of emotion, I said, "Well, why don't we try a few medications to help her heart failure? But you know what 'everything' means, don't you? I assume you don't really want us to resuscitate your grandmother?" She knew as well as I did how aggressive a procedure this was.

The young nurse turned on me angrily. She insisted that *everything,* everything possible must be done to save her grandmother. How dare I suggest that we provide anything less than that?

Angry, and feeling bound to defend the grandmother's wishes, I asked the nurse if she knew of her grandmother's advance directives, which she was clearly violating. She repeated her demands that everything be done to keep Rogers alive.

I said, "If you really love your grandmother, you'll take her home and let her die in peace." Then I walked out of the hospital and asked my senior resident to take over the case.

Mrs. Rogers was admitted to the coronary care unit and medicated. There she suffered another heart attack. I was called to her side for a code blue. I watched as a resident physician compressed the patient's tiny chest while a ventilation tube was placed in her throat. Her chest heaved up and down as the ventilator breathed for her mechanically. She remained attached to the breathing machine for several days, her dazed eyes wide open, staring out into the intensive care unit. Four days after admission, she developed pneumonia, and three days after that her heart stopped again. Another resuscitation was attempted to restart her heart; when this one failed, everyone left the room dejected.

I was responsible for pronouncing the patient, which meant calling the family to inform them of her death and then filling out the death certificate, the eighth one I had completed that day.

I thought about Mrs. Rogers's explicit request not to be resuscitated, and how her granddaughter's failure came from the fact that her feelings for her grandmother were too attached to her own needs.

What Dr. Tobin learned in this early experience emphasizes a number of lessons for this chapter. Unfortunately, having a close relative (the granddaughter) who has not discussed a person's end-of-life wishes can get in the way of doing the "right thing." In this case, Mrs. Rogers's granddaughter was "too attached to her own needs." The two daughters *should* have stood up for their mother's advance directives, but that takes guts and experience. Finally, the old rule is that if anything can go wrong—it will. Knowing this in advance, and planning for it, can often make things come out right.

9

MATTERS OF MIND AND SPIRIT

Earlier in this book, we said that two of the questions people ask when life is winding down are *Was my life worth it?* and *What's the meaning of it all?* How can you answer, or even approach, such questions when you are emotionally or physically torn apart by illness? The answer is that you need help from those around you.

This chapter is about emotional and spiritual suffering and how it can be at least in part alleviated. From the outset, we want to emphasize that "spiritual" is not the same as "religious," though people often use the terms interchangeably. At the same time, it is true that the clergy—men and women whose daily work is in specific religions—can often help us to deal with spiritual issues in a nonreligious way.

Let's start with a story.

A round of chemotherapy had produced less than promising results for Tom Bradshaw, sixty-one. Doctors said that his esophageal cancer had grown, and new cancers had appeared in his liver and stomach. Tom decided that he did not want to spend his final days in a losing battle with a rapidly advancing and very painful disease. He preferred to be as comfortable as possible and at home.

Tom and his wife, Mimi, contacted a local Miami hospice organization that helped them set up the range of services Tom would need through what turned out to be his final two months of his life. The hospice assigned a nurse and a physician to Tom's case. The hospice staff trained Mimi, their friends, and their family in administering Tom's pain medications and using tiny ice chips to help him cope with an extremely dry throat and mouth. The hospice nurse also taught Mimi how to tell when Tom's pain was increasing, so that he could be given a higher dosage of morphine to bring him comfort. In addition, Tom received visits from a family psychologist to discuss death and how to make peace with his son, with whom he had a strained relationship.

In his last meeting with the psychologist, Tom said, "I don't want to die, but it seems to be my time. It'll be okay." When the hospice nurse estimated that Tom would probably die in about two days, she told Mimi to alert family and friends who lived at a distance, so that they would have time to visit with him and say good-bye. In those two days, Tom was surrounded by a round-the-clock vigil of those who loved him. Later, many said they felt good about the way Tom died. They were grateful for the opportunity to be part of a courageous, peaceful, and graceful death in the comfort and familiar surroundings of Tom's home. A social worker from the hospice kept in touch with Mimi for a year after Tom's death, helping her to cope with her feelings of loss.

Emotional Turmoil

Caught in an emotional morass, fearful that the end is near even when it may not be, many people retreat into a private world of denial, sorrow, and intemperate images of impending disaster. We wonder about our relationships with family and friends. We wish but may not seek forgiveness and comfort. Because of this, people often do not avail themselves of the opportunity to be consoled and comforted. Especially if the end is *not* near, if they have many years yet to live—if this is merely one of those in-between taps on the shoulder—emotional distress can lead to continuing missed opportunities for comfort and joy in the years ahead.

Hope and Hopelessness

Physicians and social workers who deal with severely ill people point out that knowing when to shift gears can be very important. If your sense of hope gets mixed up with "I want a miracle," you can effectively cut yourself off from planning for the future. If, of course, you give up hope when there is still a good chance for recovery, for remission, for long life, then you are making your own life more miserable than it needs to be.

For those whose disease is chronic, hopelessness can be poisonous, since chronic illness can go on and on for years without any threat of terminal illness. For those who are acutely ill, some hope, perhaps for more limited goals—such as another visit with a grandchild, a pain-free exit, completing a painting—mixed with reality, is often the only way that people stay on an even keel psychologically.

What is not helpful, however, is false hope that is promoted by others and intended to make you feel better, for it can keep you from dealing with very important emotional and spiritual communication with your doctors and your loved ones.

Communication between patient and physician, between patient and family members, between patient and friends, clergy, social workers, psychotherapists, even strangers encountered at the doctor's office or hospital can all bring enlightenment and hope to what otherwise may seem like a dark and impossible day.

Conversations about an illness with family and friends help everybody manage. When those closest to a patient understand the illness, they are better prepared for what might come. The changes they might see in the person become easier to cope with. Also, giving updates and explaining symptoms supplies family and friends with the necessary tools for supporting their loved one.

Lukas's Story

I cannot imagine what it would have been like if I did not acknowledge to my family that cancer was a life-threatening disease, if I had said, "Hey, it's no big deal; we found it early and I'm just fine, thank you," while, underneath, terror (and that is not too strong a word to describe my feelings) ran rampant. It helped that in the middle of the night, when I woke with images of my deathbed, I could poke my wife and ask her to share my fears with me. Sure, some benefit derives from denial and down-playing. But fear can run riot in your blood and brain, sabotaging spirit and function. By admitting my fears, and by seeking help from a psychotherapist as well as my family, I was able to get through the fears into treatment, and beyond treatment into remission.

And when the second and third time came around, I was better prepared than before to share feelings, to communicate with my physicians, and to face the fears.

The support I received from my family was extraordinary.

———————————

Talking to family, physicians, friends—all of that can give you a sense of balance between what you think is reality and what may seem like foolish hope. Even if your immune system doesn't benefit from knowing that you have the love and support of friends and family, your emotional insides do. It's not always a question of whether you will get better physically from communicating about your mortality, but whether it can improve your outlook on life.

Even for those for whom the news is not as good as it was for Lukas, for those who can foresee a longer course of treatment or the closing-down of life, unburdening oneself to loved ones draws parties nearer to each other and gives them a chance to deal with the mysteries and pain of death.

Only Connect

Being open to others is valuable both for the person who is ill and the people who listen and are available to help *by* listening. For family members, friends, and, yes, for healthcare workers, too, this communication, this openness, can provide exactly the milieu that is needed to lift death beyond the "dying whimper" to the level of a fulfilling series of emotional and psychological moments.

But, surely, that's a lot easier if you're just an observer, someone who can leave the room and go on living your life. What about the dying person and the family members? It turns out that often those who are closest to the dying person, whether it be family or hospice workers, find themselves participating in a liberating and uplifting experience, a true reconciliation, a peaceful resolution. Beautiful things can happen.

When I work with people who are dying, and with their family members, I'm walking with them in the light of someone's imminent death. It's quite often a transforming experience for everybody involved. I see people really ask themselves some very significant questions about their lives and how they lived and how they will die.

—Stacie Pinderhughes, M.D.

Whether in the hospital or not, treated at home by hospice nurses or in a nursing home, each patient needs to find a way of dealing with serious disease. Each has to adjust to changing expectations and outcomes, often by changing his or her goals. Each has to find a way of living with disappointment and fear. And each has to come to terms with twists of fate and unpleasant prognoses. So the support that is given by a medical team needs to be supplemented by other caregivers, by hospice, by clergy, social workers—because one source of care is not nearly enough.

We need to create interdisciplinary teams to provide complete care, because we have every reason to be humble about what we, as physicians, can do and every reason to rely on our colleagues from the religious avenues, from the social work avenues, from pharmacological avenues. Everybody has an important place in that interdisciplinary team, including the family member. The family member is part of this interdisciplinary team.

—Linda Emanuel, M.D.,
director of Educating Physicians about End of Life Care

This fits perfectly with what one dying woman, Kathryn Meshenberg, said to those around her as she faced the last years of her life:

There are different ways that people deal with this. For me, I believe facing a life-threatening illness alone is one of the worst things imaginable, so my approach is to line up the best team I can find to support me—a medical team, a spiritual team, different kinds of medicines, family, friends, and colleagues. You say to yourself, yes, this is a big deal, but I'll be able to do it. And my job is to be as open as possible. I see this as a piece of cloth or a tapestry, a tapestry of care. If you close your eyes and imagine a beautiful mosaic tapestry, it's woven of many, many strands, and the strands represent all the different elements that help me every single day. My husband, my children, my grandchildren, the rest of my family, friends, my rabbi, Western medicine, Chinese medicine, Ayurvedic medicine, my meditation group—all are a part of my tapestry. Also woven in are prayers from people sending their best wishes and their positive thoughts, as well as my own. It's a big combination of things and every time something is added to the tapestry, I feel as though I have one more opportunity to stay healthy for as long as possible.

The Family

What does that mean, that the family member is a part of the team? What, in the midst of their grief, can family members do? First of all, they can transmit patient wishes directly and forcefully. The patient, after all, is the very center of the team. Then, it turns out that it is not so much what family members *do* as it is what a family can *be* as it comes together over the end of life of a loved one or friend. If, as this book has attempted to persuade you, you can admit that someone you care about is really dying, then you can participate in that person's last months and days in a way that allows everyone in the family to benefit from the experience. And we mean everyone: the dying person, as well.

What kind of participation? Your presence, your openness to accept death as a part of life, your willingness to forgive, and your openness to be forgiven:

"I forgive you."

"Forgive me."

"Thank you."

"Good-bye."

Four powerful phrases, a mantra originated by Dr. Ira Byock, a pioneer in hospice care. Whether these words are spoken in just this fashion is not the point. What is important is that a pathway of communication be opened from the first day of diagnosis (months or years before) through to the last day of life; that we, as mortal human beings, admit that mortality to each other and say to each other the important things we have left unsaid.

You may ask what you need to forgive, but deep within each of us there is always that frightened corner of life in which we fear we have done something harmful to another human being, often a family member. To forgive a dying person for that unspoken but bitter experience is to lift a weight, perhaps one you did not know you carried.

Many people find that saying what they want to say can be an enormous relief for everyone in the family. That doesn't mean you should necessarily accuse your dying brother of ruining your life, or leave your son with guilt after you have died. It does mean that you should feel free to gently open those hidden sore spots that may have kept you from showing your love and concern over the years. Almost every family has such areas, and people who die very often need to open themselves to forgive or ask for forgiveness or to speak the powerful words that give comfort to those left behind.

Of course, there are other things that comfort. Two sisters, long estranged, may find that they can tell each other how much they've missed the other; a son and father may exchange words of familial love. It's all a way of providing what's called "closure."

Comfort comes in a wide variety of forms. When the folksinger Pete Seeger's aunt was dying, a goodly number of members of his family stood around the bed in the hospital. There may have been ten or twelve of them, all ages. They sang songs that the dying woman remembered and loved from her childhood and from her days in that musical family. We are told it was a peaceful death, as peaceful as any of them had ever seen. And we can imagine the sense of calm and emotional togetherness that it gave to those who stood around that bed.

Family members should not be afraid to touch those who are ill or dying. Time and again, when given a chance to touch and be touched—physically and emotionally—at the end of life, the air is cleared, and the whole feeling of the death can be changed.

Lukas's Story

When I got lymphoma, my family rallied around. On weekends, our two daughters (22 and 24) came up from the city to have brunch with us or just hang out. They kept track of my radiation treatments, called to see how I was. When it was useful for any of the four of us to talk about the disease process, we did that. When we wanted to forget about it and talk about other matters, we did that.

Like many men (fathers or not), I had tended to fend off being taken care of. I felt that I didn't "need" it. During my treatment for cancer, however, my daughters and my wife were definitely put in the position of taking care of me—and I let them. My wife read up on what food would be best to eat, and what exercise would be helpful. She contacted the American Cancer Society. She went on the Internet. And it was a wonderful experience to feel that I could just let go.

As it turned out, this cancer did not become deadly. But if it had, and when cancer came my way again, what a shame it would have been to have robbed us of the time together to talk and forgive. If I had not been willing to admit death was knocking, those blessings would have been gone.

Bringing a family to a point where every difficult step is discussed, planned for, and taken together can be a difficult task. But there is support available for doing this, and the reward for overcoming fears about talking is great.

Think, too, what a feeling for our daughters: that they could look after the father who had spent many years taking care of them. If I had not let them do that, I would have robbed them of an opportunity to make themselves feel like "good" daughters, to be helpful. And I would have robbed myself of the opportunity for all of us to get closer.

Coworkers

Let's go back to the diagnosis. Throughout the book, we have suggested that diagnosis isn't the same as dying; that *having* cancer is not the same as *being dead* from cancer. Yes, your cancer may kill you in the end, but for now you are very much alive and need all the support you can muster to fight the disease, to remain a living creature, not a dead one, to be a person, not just a patient.

One of the ways to do this is to use every sphere of your daily life to keep you on track. Obviously, since most of us work, and most of us do not immediately give up that work when we have a diagnosis, the workplace is one crucial arena to seek support and to give support.

Having a life-threatening illness in the workplace has its own unique difficulties. It might be harder to be open with coworkers who are not personal friends. There might be fears, for the patient and her colleagues, that quality of work will suffer. But the rule of thumb, talking as openly as possible, still applies. It is the best way to create an environment that is supportive and productive.

> What I found to be incredibly important is to talk to my colleagues, my team members, and my staff about my diagnosis. As soon as I got it, and recovered from the bad news, I talked to everybody in our team. It was to let them know, and to give them permission to talk to me about my disease. When I did that, they also gave me permission to talk more about it. And from that open dialogue came more support in the workplace. I think that we need to talk more about illness and death in workplaces everywhere. It's terrible to have this sort of disease or any life-limiting disease and not be able to talk about it to people with whom you work, or with whom you have any kind of enduring commerce.
>
> —Kathryn (Kit) Meshenberg

Are there dangers in this approach? What if the team decides you're no longer capable of carrying on your duties when *you* believe you are? What if people find your openness distracting and difficult and impeding their own emotional life?

Obviously, each person has to gauge his or her own workplace for these possibilities. Perhaps you should discuss the policy of openness first with your supervisor or boss. In the case of Meshenberg, later discussions proved that she was right about being open, right about how she handled it.

She approached her supervisor and said, in essence, "I want to live with a life-threatening illness in the workplace, if you don't mind." She was open about where she was physically and emotionally.

Later on, one of her coworkers said, "What made it easier is that you took the lead to help us to know what was going on. I thought it was easier to know how to respond to you, because you'd say, this is what's going on today, or this is how I feel about talking about this. And it was so easy for us—if you hadn't done that, it would have been a lot more difficult."

And Meshenberg herself said, "It was only by giving that I could get back cues on how things could work together, and how people were feeling."

It's a juggling act on all sides. Coworkers themselves should ask how much they should be proactive in discussing the illness. Experts suggest the following:

- Let the ill person make the first move. If he or she doesn't open up, there's probably a good reason, and you should let it go at that.
- You might start simply, by saying (assuming the news is public), "I heard some bad things about your health. I'm sorry." If your coworker does want to go further, give him or her the chance to do so.
- Be aware that there are many ups and downs in any illness. A person may be in shock after the first diagnosis, but then take on full responsibilities of his/her job.
- Sometimes radiation or medications can cause momentary lapses in judgment. If this happens, it's not untoward to gently tell your coworker about this.
- On the other hand, nothing says that because your coworker is ill and wants to keep going that you should have to be burdened with more than your share. Be open about this, as you are open about other feelings.

Lukas's Story _____

At work, colleagues accepted my initial unwillingness to discuss details of the illness with them, but they were enthusiastic about my willingness to go on with my tasks, even during the roughest radiation treatments. And it helped me to do so, made me feel that I was *not* terribly ill, that I was still a person, not just a patient.

When the second and third cancer diagnoses came around, I changed my mind. Anyone who wanted to hear about my illness— *anyone*—got an earful. I wanted all the emotional support I could find!

_____

Social Workers and Other Counselors

There often comes a time when you may feel so sad or angry or anxious about your illness that you cannot be consoled. You cannot get up in the morning, you cannot face your friends; you cannot talk about feelings to family members who are eager to help. If you choose to continue to work, life seems so heavy, work so meaningless, that it's almost impossible to function.

This can happen to you; it can happen to your friends and family; it can even happen to caregivers. Whomever it happens to, it is clearly a time when intervention by trained personnel is valuable.

It is, of course, not surprising that your impending death or that of someone you care about should cause grief. But if it also causes depression or anxiety beyond what might be normally expected, some counseling is needed.

Now, you may not believe in psychotherapy. You may feel that it is a wasted effort at this time. After all, a therapist can't prolong your life; a social worker can't bring your health back. True enough. But a supportive and empathic therapist can make you feel more secure in what you're doing, can help you cope with the losses you're encountering, and can help you justify your actions and feelings to yourself. It helps tremendously to know that you are *not* overreacting, that you are *not* being too emotional, that your experiences inside do match what's happening to you in the real world. Knowing that others have gone through these events with similar feelings can normalize the experience. And you can certainly get encouragement for continuing a path you have decided to take in the midst of this catastrophe that is happening to you.

Finding someone to give you psychological support is not as tricky or difficult as some believe.

- You might start by asking friends and relatives whether they've had anyone who was particularly successful in helping them.
- Many health care institutions of any size have a staff or attendant social worker or psychologist, most of whom are particularly tuned to the problems of people with serious illnesses. If you haven't already been assigned one, ask for one.
- Almost every community has a clinic where emotional counseling can be found.
- There are 3,000 hospices in America, one near enough to you to at least consider your needs. You don't have to be a patient with them in order to solicit their help in solving your emotional dilemmas.

Here's how one such professional came to Lukas's aid in a crisis.

Lukas's Story

When I was diagnosed with prostate cancer, I had just turned sixty-five. I had switched over to Medicare but due to a stupid misunderstanding on my part, I had not opted for outpatient reimbursement. I just wasn't thinking.

My prostate cancer was treated with external radiation. It was very expensive. I assumed the bills were going to Medicare. They were, but they were rejected because this was *outpatient* treatment. Looking back on it, I realized that I'd actually told Medicare by letter that I *did* want the optional coverage, but because they were backlogged with computer glitches, they didn't switch me on until long after my treatment began. Which meant that I would need to pay the thousands of dollars of treatment costs ($19,000 I believe was the final figure) *myself.*

It was bad enough having cancer a second time; worse to have to go daily for forty days for radiation. But the fact that I might have screwed myself up with this insurance business—at a time when I didn't know if renewed cancer would prevent me from ever working again—was the end of the road. I went into a deep depression, alternating with wild anxiety.

Nothing my wife or friends could say was any solace. Sure, I was aware that my emotional turmoil was, at least in part, due not to financial difficulties, but to the mere fact that I had cancer again. Sure, we could eventually pay the money if we had to. Sure, I could make a deal with the hospital to pay off over time. Sure, sure, sure! But none of that counted. None of that worked to assuage my feelings.

In short, I was in an emotional bind caused by all the factors of assault we've talked about in this book: I thought I was dying, and this money foul-up was the straw that finally broke my back.

One day, after receiving radiation at the hospital, it occurred to me that there must be some kind of psychological support available. In fact, there were a number of social workers trained in support psychotherapy at the hospital, and I phoned one. She agreed to see me the next day.

For several weeks, while I battled with Medicare over its computers and battled with the hospital's financial people (whose blood seemed to be iced each morning in order to keep them from acknowledging my terror), I took forty minutes off every so often to sit in a little office with an amazing woman whose job was to soothe the emotional turmoil of cancer patients.

What did she do for me?

- She *validated* for me that my emotional train wreck was not a sign of going crazy, but rather a very understandable reaction to trauma.
- She agreed that both Medicare and the hospital were behaving badly.
- She told me how often the mere diagnosis of cancer or other serious illnesses can upset patients emotionally and spiritually, even if death is far, far away.
- She set to work to understand what personal factors existed that were preventing me from getting my fears under control.

In other words, she worked on the general and on the specific: the factors that affect *every* patient, and those that were particular to *me*.

Within a few weeks, I was calm enough to go about my daily work. I could, once again, sit down and have a quiet dinner with my wife. And, equally important, I regained enough of my smarts to get on the phone with a U.S. senator's office to get them to intervene with Medicare. Shortly thereafter, a letter arrived from Medicare, admitting their goof (not mine) and saying they'd pay for everything incurred at the hospital.

No, my cancer didn't go away—and there was nothing the social worker could do to help me there—but in some sense I was reborn: I found strengths and renewed emotional (and physical) energy from sharing my feelings with someone else, with someone who could help me see through the tunnel to the light.

Grief and Closure

Of course, with anyone's death, there is still grief, there is disbelief, there is true sorrow. But when underlying, unspoken questions and accusations that are part of any family's history are out in the open, when forgiveness and touching (both emotional and physical) are possible, psychological burdens can lift. A close feeling is created that would not have been possible, a legacy of emotional support that might not have occurred otherwise. One young man whose brother died of AIDS described the course of the disease like this: "We got really close together. We cried a lot. We laughed some, too. That was the best time for my brother and me and my family."

What this suggests is that beyond comfort, there can be actual closure at the end of life. *Closure* is a word that has become distorted and cheapened by its constant usage in too many situations, but it does have a very important meaning when it comes to grief. Closure is necessary not only for the family, but for the dying person, too. What many people don't realize is that it is not only those left behind who are grieving. When we are ill, when we have lost a piece of ourselves (a breast, a part of our colon, a lung), even though we may yet live a long time, we, too, grieve.

If we have lost the ability to function in some areas, or if we are too ill to go out to the symphony or to play with friends, or if we fear that life itself will be taken away, our grief can be enormous.

Closure can occur when we admit these feelings to ourselves and when we share them with our caretakers, our family, our friends. Crying in front of those we love can be painful, as if we are revealing a soft, undefended part of ourselves but it can also be a wonderful release. We share our grief with those who will have to grieve with us or after us, and the mutual feelings support us all. Men, often self-protected against such feelings, can find special relief in sharing them with buddies or spouse or children.

When Dylan Thomas wrote, "Do not go gentle into that good night," he was asking us to rage against death. Rage, cry, feel your loss, share it with others, and it can lessen the pain. It is human to do so, and can give others a sense that you and they share humanity.

Just Being Present

For caregivers—family, friends, health professionals—sometimes talking isn't even necessary. Just being there, present at the bedside, sends a message that you care, that you want to give part of yourself. A touch on the hand, tears on your face, your very warmth can make a difference in allowing the dying person to go through what he or she needs to go through in order to die. David, a cancer patient, felt that way. Here's how he put it:

The simplest thing for anybody to do—to me—would be at times just to be there. Not necessarily to do or say anything, just to be there. I can feel you there. I want you to be there.

Honesty of feelings is a precious commodity that can open up lines of communication between those we love and those by whom we are cherished. While it is painful to leave this earth and painful to have others leave us, it is even more painful not to have said good-bye.

Spiritual Support

When death is certain—and often when it is still far away—men and women look backward, trying to put their lives into perspective, to figure out whether they have accomplished what they wanted to accomplish. Doing this formally is called a "life review," but whether it's done formally or just in a casual way, it can be very helpful to people at the end of their lives. It almost always gives them a sense that their life was worth living.

Which bring us to matters of the spirit.

We suggested at the beginning of this chapter that it is natural for people saddled with chronic, debilitating illnesses and for those nearing the end of life to ask some rather enormous questions about life. Often, this takes courage. Often, too, people feel there is no point in asking questions to which the answers seem far away or impossible to obtain, questions such as *What's the meaning of it all?* Or *Is God punishing me?* Or *Why?*

But it is hard to come to the end of life without wanting to make something cohesive of your experience and of your presence for all the years you've lived. These journeys into meaning have a spiritual coloration to them. Dying people who can put some spiritual meaning to their life apparently die more peacefully.

What is meant by "spiritual"? Most people seem to know what *they* mean when they say spiritual, but not what *others* mean. Some think it's about "religion," some mean "matters beyond the physical," and some think spiritual means anything that's not in the here and now; some simply mean things that are of the psychological realm. The whole area is complicated and very individual. For the purposes of this chapter we use the term to mean those things that go into realms where we do not have answers and where we crave them, matters of value and mystery. For many, these are religious matters; for others, they're existential dilemmas. It doesn't matter what you call them: recognizing their existence is what's important.

There are many questions people ask, such as, "Why me?" "Why am I the one who is given this burden?" Whether that's a reasonable question to ask doesn't matter; whether it can be answered or not doesn't matter. It pops into our minds. Did we do something wrong in the eyes of God to be given this painful news? Another spiritual question, one that comes later on for most of us, is, "What is the meaning of existence if it can be challenged in such a shocking way?"

By now you can see that we are into existential questions of a monumental order. These issues cry out to be addressed. The "why me?" or "what is this suffering for?" kind of question seems particularly impenetrable. Experts, however, say that the important thing is to have the courage to state those kinds of questions, that seeking answers can be almost as fulfilling as receiving them.

"The dying soul is filled with terror," one minister told us. People want to know why this is happening. They want to eliminate the spiritual pain: the thought, perhaps, that they are being punished for something done earlier in life—for sin. The family wants to know why their loved one is suffering. The patient feels out of control, unloved, unwanted.

There is the fear of the unknown, the fate of the human soul. Even asking such questions, let alone trying to answer them, requires dialogue with someone. Which brings us to another of those conversations that we have urged people to have. What's the point of such conversations?

- To establish that there is a component of our being that goes beyond the physical—simply to acknowledge that.
- To dispel some misconceptions ("This is not God's punishment").
- To give individuals a chance to explore areas of doubt, disbelief, and concern that may not be explored in any other arena.
- To permit courage to replace anxiety wherever possible.

Though Western medicine has, over time, separated physical care from patients' spiritual needs, there is increasing recognition of the importance of spirituality in the care of dying people. Numerous studies support the important role spirituality plays in patient care. When medicine confronts life-limiting illness in particular, and when cure becomes less likely, it is of paramount importance to help patients cope with their suffering and eventual dying.

Physicians and other health care providers increasingly recognize that good care of dying people is as much or more about these questions as it is about the relief of pain and other symptoms. Spirituality is an expression of how people relate to a larger whole—something greater than themselves—and how they find meaning in the midst of their suffering. Our elderly population is increasing, and as our family members and friends grow ill and die, the experience becomes vivid to every one of us.

Many hospitals recognize the role of spiritual caring in their provisions for chaplains and religious services and the inclusion of chaplains or other religious advisers on palliative care teams. Hospice has long recognized the critical importance of involving pastoral professionals on interdisciplinary teams and always makes this service part of the total package of care available to all patients and their families. And even medical schools are realizing that addressing spirituality can be an important and useful part of patient care and doctors' own well-being.

While some doctors and nurses may hesitate to tread on spiritual ground, it seems that Americans want their doctors to ask them about spiritual concerns. In 1996, *USA Today* reported that 63 percent of people surveyed believe it is good for doctors to talk to patients about spiritual beliefs.

A Wide Variety of Comfort Is Available

It might seem that members of the clergy would be the most helpful at times like these. But if spiritual support came only in the form of clergy assistance during one's last moments, or in rote repeating of hoary myths, most Americans say they wouldn't want it. They do want spiritual support, but not necessarily religious input. Which brings up the question of just who should be involved in these scenes at the end of life.

> Those of us who do work in this field have come to understand that this is a journey that is taken not just by the individual involved, but by all of those around him. There is an opportunity, but there are also, of course, issues that arise. What sometimes happens is that the family doesn't quite journey together. Often, as end of life approaches, the patient is perhaps farther along on that journey than family members

are. And sometimes even family members, through very good intentions—through the best of intentions—through love and fear and devotion—hold back that person from their journey. Or sometimes just the opposite—push them a little too fast. This is where those of us who work in this field really can make a wonderful contribution. Our task is not just to help the person involved, but it is to minister to the family. Just as the patient has to confront their own issues, as best they can, with honesty, courage, and openness, so do the family members. There are wonderful opportunities for the family to take this journey together. And grow as a family.

—Douglas Sagal, rabbi, KAM-Isaiah Israel Congregation, Chicago

We don't by any means want to suggest that clergy should *not* be involved in spiritual matters at the end of life. They have, in fact, been thinking about these matters for their entire careers. But if, for whatever reason, the particular clergy with whom you are used to dealing do not provide the kind of spiritual support you want and need, it doesn't mean you can't find it. In fact, there are as many different kinds of spiritual advisers and ways to seek spiritual solace as there are people seeking advice and comfort. For instance:

- *Clergy members—a priest, pastor, rabbi, imam.* Over the past few years, many of these men and women have been joining the end-of-life education movement, going back to relearn how to approach spiritual issues, and not necessarily as religious issues, but learning how to listen creatively.
- *Instrospection.* Over the centuries people have sought to come to terms with the universe, whether that be through meditation, prayer, or going to a religious institution on the Sabbath.
- *Family members.* Talking to a parent, child, or more distant relative about spiritual matters may be just the right way to air issues. "Are we doing the right thing?" "Aren't we hastening death by withholding care?" These questions have a spiritual, not just an ethical or practical dimension.
- *Rituals.* You may find that the rituals that accompany religious observances have a very soothing effect, even on nonbelievers. If you're normally put off by what may seem the rote quality or affectation or "meaninglessness" of a religious rite, you may find it that affects you differently at a time of need. Some people find that the group service or ancient words of a ritual can comfort them now, even though earlier in life they found them without meaning.

We all have questions. Finding answers is the hard part. In twenty-first century America, while most Americans profess a belief in a supreme being, and most go to church or synagogue or mosque, even if only on special occasions, the fact is that those same people may not find comfort in the standard answers of years past. It may be that "We have no answer" or "God knows best" or "Have faith" or "This is the way" is not enough for you when you're a dying person or struck by a severe illness. If that is so, you may have to find your own pathway to spiritual understanding or comfort, or you may simply have to look harder to find the clergyman or woman who can help you come to terms.

This can be especially important during your last months, weeks, and days. Or you may simply have come to the decision that there *is* no understanding, and that you don't want clergy around you. Whatever your choice, it is clearly yours to make. This is one place where you will want to listen to your family and friends about their feelings, but you will want to make the decision yourself.

> I do think that I've developed a real appreciation for understanding the value and importance of attending to the spiritual needs of people. I can't answer questions about the meaning of life and death very effectively, but I can sure tell you, with plenty of emphasis, that people who are able to have some time—through religion, meditation, anything— to understand the spiritual component of being human beings do much better in regards to comfort, pain control, and making the most of end of life.
>
> —Michael Preodor, M.D.

The Dialogue

So how should people—whether clergy, health care professionals, or family members—address these issues? How do such dialogues take place? We asked a number of people, both in and outside the clergy, and got remarkably similar responses.

- It's crucial that you let the patient know you're willing to talk about this dying stuff. You may need to actually say that to them.

- The Dalai Lama is said to have defined love as wanting to make someone happy and compassion as wanting to reduce someone's suffering. It seems to us that compassion is what is wanted here, and sometimes the most important listener can be a compassionate outsider, a witness, someone who doesn't have a stake in the outcome of this conversation.

- Your primary role is not to give answers, nor even to raise questions, but to *be* there, to be a reflecting mirror in which the patient can see his or her own thoughts and feelings, so be willing to just listen. Even though you may have strong feelings, unless the patient wants to hear them, let his or her thoughts be primary. For instance, when someone says, "I'm being punished by God," it's hard not to counter with "Don't be ridiculous!" or "No, you're a good person." It may be better to acknowledge that many of us feel that way, or to ask why the patient feels he or she should be punished. Or—and this is even harder—just listen and witness that spiritual pain.

- If, on the other hand, your opinion is solicited ("But what do *you* think abut this?"), try to offer alternatives, not firm dogma that may be "true" to you, but not necessarily to the patient. You might try saying, "Well, I've looked at it this way . . ." or "I was talking to so-and-so the other day, and he said he thought . . ."

- Often a person may engage in dialogue simply to have a way of venting feelings, not really to find answers. Be sensitive to this possibility. One psychologist told us that people often need to feel that you, the listener, are there for the bad stuff as well as the good; that being willing to hear about the patient's spiritual pain may be the most valuable thing you can do.

- Let the patient decide when enough is enough, to terminate the discussion.

Lucas's experience may offer some guides to how both sides of this dialogue might go.

Lukas's Story

A woman from the chaplain's office at Sloan-Kettering came to my room after the surgery for bowel resection. She was a former psychotherapist who was undergoing training as a rabbi. I didn't tell her that I was not a practicing Jew, rather, I waited to see what she might offer. After all, I had been told three times that I had cancer. Fate was hanging around. I was sixty-eight years old, and I had fears aplenty.

She asked me if I wanted to talk. I said why not.

It was clear from the beginning that she had no firm answers. She couldn't say whether or not "God" knew or planned or even thought about my pain and my anxiety.

But she did think that it was valuable for me to talk, even if I didn't believe in God or in rabbis as great helpers in general.

I said, "I've been tapped on the shoulder three times now, and it's getting to the point where I'm pretty sure that I'll eventually die from cancer of one sort or another. What should I do?"

She said, "What do you *want* to do?"

I said that I wanted to keep working, that I had lots of plans, lots of projects, miles to go before the end of my list. "I've decided to do some acting now—mainly Shakespeare—and I'm writing a book, and my daughter's getting married . . . and . . ."

"Sounds good," she said.

As I sat there in bed listening to her ask questions, I realized that on one level it didn't matter what she asked, or what she said. What mattered was that someone was listening, and that I was talking, exploring what I was afraid of, what hung over my shoulder.

"Someday I'm going to die," I said.

"We're all going to die," she said.

I said that wasn't a really helpful remark. I didn't *want* to die, and that was what upset me, not that I was singled out for this plight. "Though I r*eally* don't like the fact that I've been given an *earlier* death sentence."

Maybe, she suggested, it would help to think of all that I might be able to accomplish before death actually happens. And maybe that very effort can help me accomplish some things that are very important.

"I think that's true," I said.

"Are you frightened?"

"No more than the first time. Perhaps less."

"That's good. That should free you do to more things."

"Okay, I've been reprieved—yet again."

Then I asked her what there was that she could *do* for me.

"I could pray for you," she said, and to my surprise I agreed.

"O *Source,*" she said, and smiled at me (in acknowledgment of my skepticism about God's existence). "O Source of all health: give Christopher Lukas—whom you already know—" (again, the smile) "—the ability to continue in better health, so he can accomplish those things he wants and needs to accomplish."

Well, that was simple. And it did help.

One more note: While I was carrying on this conversation, in the next cubicle, a man was receiving communion from two young women from his church who had come in to see him. Their voices were like chants in counterpoint to my quiet conversation, and I realized at that moment how diverse and strange are the ways to receive comfort.

Laughter

We want to end with something that has become a theme in several of our chapters: the power of laughter. We want to suggest to you that, putting the theoretical question of its "curative" powers aside, comedy and laughter can simply be wonderful distractions from pain, sorrow, and fear. If it turns out that laughing can also strengthen the immune system, so much the better. But for now, remember that while you and a patient are laughing, they can't also be crying; that pain can be assuaged by laughter; and, if nothing else, that laughter can distract you from the fears of the moment.

And that's powerful emotional medicine!

Summing Up

Receiving bad news can be traumatic. Being told that you've got a serious disease, whether chronic, acute, or terminal, can shake your fundamental belief in the universe. And even if it doesn't unnerve you completely, it can certainly spoil your enjoyment in life and your relationships with others, not to mention your ability to function as you would wish to function.

Whether this is a condition that will be short-lived or long-term, you will want to come to terms with it. So, we believe you should consider *all* of the supports—the "tapestry of care" that we've discussed in this chapter. Only you can decide which are most important: whether you need and can get help from a social worker or other psychotherapist; whether you want pastoral counseling; whether you and your spouse of thirty or forty years need to sit down and trade forgiveness; whatever you choose.

But one thing is certain: the more you bury your feelings and doubts and wishes, the harder it will be in the long run for you to provide yourself with the ability to carry on with life—and whether that life is another thirty years or just thirty days, you will want to be able to make it valuable to yourself and those around you.

10

CAREGIVERS

If we have led you to assume that it is easy for family and friends—or for any *caregivers*—to attend to someone who is dying, we want to correct the impression. It isn't as if you can just wander in and out of a loved one's hospital room or hospice and assimilate it into your life. Eighty percent of hospice care is at home, where husbands, wives, and grown children are the *primary* caregivers—doing duty twenty-four hours a day, seven days a week. It's time-consuming and difficult. And that doesn't even include all the patients with non-terminal, but chronic diseases who are taken care of at home by a combination of relatives and paid (or volunteer) community caregivers.

In short, our discussion has not taken into account nor done justice to the stress that a family caregiver goes through, nor what can be done about it. That's what this chapter is about.

It is tough enough to be the spouse or daughter or friend of someone who is chronically ill, even on an on-again, off-again basis. But when the patient becomes homebound (even when receiving hospice care), roles of family members begin to change. As illness progresses, those close to the patient find themselves filling the much-needed role of a caregiver: giving medication, providing help for accomplishing everyday things, coordinating with the medical team and hospice workers, and just being nearby. The number of such caregivers has increased enormously. When Medicare adopted the home hospice benefit, family after family found itself taking care of very ill people, seldom with the training or comprehension of what that entailed beforehand.

It is estimated that as many as 25 million people provide care for family members in their homes. This is not just an occasional dose of medicine or a swipe with a cold cloth across a loved one's brow. Many if not most of America's caregivers do the shopping, take the patient to the hospital or physician's office, bathe and dress the patient, feed, clean . . . all of it, often giving up their own private and professional lives during the process.

According to Carol Levine, one of the most articulate and informed of the advocates on caregiving, "Nearly 83 percent of caregivers have *no paid professional help.*" That means no nurses, physical therapists, social workers, or home health aides. In some ways, this is a national scandal, hiding a crisis of its own behind other health care statistics.

Many people who take on the caregiving role don't take into consideration the wide variety of disruptions in their lives.

- Someone has to take on the responsibilities of the ill person.
- Someone has to take on some of the responsibilities of the caregiver.
- Even a simple visit to the hospital during a momentary crisis can leave a caregiver emotionally and physically drained, unprepared to take on "normal" jobs at home.

These "someones" are usually the primary female resident of the household or, often, the nearest female relative or close friend available.

Caregiving is a role that requires so much from a person that it is important to share the load as much as possible. Every caregiver needs to think about how to put together a team of people to help them provide care— friends, hospice volunteers, community assets.

Even with such forethought, all too often there *is* no one else, at least temporarily. Take the story of Shirley Loflin, sole caretaker of her husband and father—both of whom had similar strokes and were living at home.

One week, our old furnace died, the plumbing backed up, the city was in the midst of a huge flood, a small tornado whirled through our neighborhood and ripped off shingles. Debris was everywhere. My husband had his first seizure and, on top of it all, Daddy [also bedbound] was upset because my husband needed so much of my attention.

The Toll

It is not the purpose of this chapter to scare people away from caregiving, but it is important that current and future caregivers recognize the enormous toll that such work takes on them, and that the public recognize what a tremendous debt we owe them.

Here are some of the hard, cold facts.

- Studies found that the psychological and physical stress on caregivers resulted in a much higher risk of them dying early—from strokes, heart attacks, or just being plain worn out.
- Among caregivers, sleep disorders, intestinal problems, and other complaints mount day by day, month by month.
- Caregiver burnout is seen at every stage of the journey. When it sets in depends on how prepared a caregiver is and how much stamina she has.
- One of the greatest burdens is that caregivers find they have little or no control over many parts of their lives, whether it is the health care system that breaks down or something as simple as not being able to get out and do the shopping.
- Guilt, resentment, fatigue, fear—all of these are present during a caregiver's day, leading to an enormous physical and mental toll. Alzheimer's is an especially wearying disease to care for, since it takes years and requires ever more vigilant caregiving.
- While women fall prey to depression and back problems, male caregivers are more likely to fall prey to substance abuse and violence.
- Finally, many caregivers do not even recognize that they are under enormous stress. When they do, they feel guilty about asking for help. As a consequence, they dig a deeper and deeper hole for themselves, physically and mentally. Without some respite or counseling, the physical and mental toll can be devastating.

Lukas's Story _____

My wife, Susan, took full charge of my life when I first got lymphoma. She saw to it that I ate well, that there was plenty of humor in our lives, and that I had visitors when I wanted them— and none when I didn't. Since I had been the cook for most of our married life, it was a great relief to have someone else do the cooking, but it put a burden on Susan, who was also carrying a full load as a psychotherapist five days a week. She was an important breadwinner in our home, and now had given herself the charge of seeing to it that I got healthy.

Well, I did get healthy—for over ten years, with the exception of my prostate cancer, which was common enough in my age group not to cause me exceptional anxiety or despair. But then I got really sick again: the lymphoma was back, and they had to operate on my abdomen to take out a potentially dangerous polyp. So there we were, back in serious worry mode. And I will confess, I did not see this as something Susan needed to worry about as much as *I* did. When I came back home and found her spacing out and not hearing what I had to say, and being especially tired, I found it more irritating than worrisome. Then, one night, a lightbulb went off in Susan's brain. She turned to me and said that she realized what was going on was a kind of traumatization. For her. She was trying to be brave and assume—as I did—that all would be well. But, deep down, she had been sandbagged by the return of the cancer; sandbagged and frightened so much that she was going through her work and her home life in a kind of numb protectiveness.

———————————

It has been only in recent years that the size and toll of caregiver stress has received some of the press attention it deserves. Rosalynn Carter, wife of the ex-president, devotes her own Rosalynn Carter Institute at Georgia Southwestern State University to the help and education of family and professional caregivers, and it is partly through her efforts and those of some grassroots groups that proper help is being directed to caregivers across the country. (See the Resources section for more on help for caregivers.)

It's lonely and stressful and frustrating. There are lots of reasons for that: Today, families are not as close as they once were. People are not having as many children as they had. Women work. And we're living much longer due to medical advances. The older the population gets, the more caregivers are going to be needed. More and more people will need care, and there are fewer and fewer people to give it. We must look closer at the problem and see what we can do for caregivers, legislatively, for one thing, but also what can be done in communities all across our country for those who are really in dire need of help. I have a friend who says that there are four kinds of caregivers, those who have been caregivers, those who are caregivers, those who will be caregivers, and those who will need caregivers. That's all of us. At one time in our lives, we're going to either need care or have to give care.

—Rosalynn Carter

To understand the depth of the problem, one has to accept the fact that the state of financing of home care and hospice care is sufficiently insecure, and the length of decline and of chronic or long-term illnesses so great, that almost no family can afford full-time care for a dying family member. This leaves many patients between home and nursing home, or between hospice and hospital, being taken care of by a daughter or niece or sister.

The Result: the so-called "sandwich generation," consisting mainly of women who must both raise their own adolescent children and serve as caretaker, nurse, and conversationalist for a parent who is sick enough to need care, but not sick enough to go into the hospital, or whose family decides that a nursing home is not suitable for their loved one.

What the Carter Institute does and what some others are beginning to do is, first, educate people about the burdens of caregiving; second, lobby for more financial help for long-term illness; third, seek to find every means possible to give caretakers some respite.

Mrs. Carter says that one of the first things is for caregivers to recognize that they are entitled to time off. The second thing is to find some way of giving them that time.

Here is where the vagaries of the Medicare law come into play. Here is where we should avail ourselves of all the knowledge we can about whether our parent or grandparent is entitled to hospice care at home, to a nurse and nurse's aide, and to a physician who will come to the home—and for whom reimbursement is available. (The law changes often. Log on to the Carter Institute or a Medicare rights group on the Web for information on the most current legislation.)

The Two Sides of Caregiving

While caregiving has many negative aspects, we want to stress that there is a positive side, too.

A little while back, we filmed at the home of a man about seventy-five who had ALS. He was chairbound and on a breathing apparatus, but he could still communicate with his wife and others through grunts and facial gestures. His wife, also in her seventies, took care of him gladly, she told us, because they had been long married, and having him at home was a blessing. There came a time, however, when she could no longer help him to and from bed or bathroom. Her local hospice provided daily care to move him from place to place, and weekly nursing or doctor help to see what his status was at the time, or to suggest new medication to relieve his symptoms. It was paid for by Medicare because his physicians felt that it was likely, under normal circumstances, for him to live no more than six months. To be sure, he had outlived that time (partly, we were told, precisely because he had such good and loving care), but the judgment of the doctors was the best they could give and Medicare supported that.

The wife told us that she was extremely grateful to the hospice for providing care, that without it she would have been unable to provide the comforts of home, and more than that, that she was grateful for the respite they gave her, so she could take time for her own needs: her physical and emotional well-being. But still, she, like many caregivers, also expressed the joy she felt at being able to make a difference in the emotional and physical well-being of her loved one.

The fact is, caregiving can be a remarkably rewarding experience. Time and again, caregivers report that they were able to establish a bond between themselves and the ill person that did not exist beforehand. It is not that the person being taken care of necessarily responds with gratitude and love for what he or she is receiving. It is that the act of caring for another human being can produce a satisfying emotional experience.

Of all the personal stories about such satisfaction, none was more poignant to us than the following from a man who has been taking care of his wife for years. She has Alzheimer's disease.

What matters is becoming aware of my role as Patti's caregiver as being privileged and rewarding. The day of the diagnosis in 1992, as we cried and hugged, I said to her, "We will do this together and it will be my privilege to be with you and take care of you." Now, I get to feel accomplished and even pride from doing tasks that need to be done; because now I am looking for a very different result from the "mechanics" of the task to an emotional and spiritual comfort. If some of these necessary tasks felt like drudgery, performing them with the purpose of creating special moments of joy can change that feeling dramatically. The joy that Patti brings to me when I see her experiencing a moment of joy is beyond my ability to describe. Often through tears, I can say thank you!

Unfortunately, of the people who died of chronic or long-term illnesses or diseases in 2000, fewer than half that number had hospice care. For those who do—and those who do not—experts in caretaking and its stresses suggest rigorous organization ahead of time as a way of reducing some of the burden. For instance:

- Get financial and medical issues in order.
- Ask the doctor questions, conduct your own research, and contact local agencies for more information about the condition you're dealing with.
- Get informed about hands-on techniques. Contact your local American Red Cross to find a caregiving class offered in your community.
- Talk it over with all family members and friends and develop a plan of care.
- Make time for yourself. All caregivers need time away; it's good for everyone.
- But remember why you're here; always respect the need for the patient's independence and his or her choices.
- Look ahead; seek out options for the day when you no longer can provide care.
- Share, share, share; a network of social support is important for everyone.
- Set limits: determine at what point you can no longer provide care.

Here's how Kit Meshenberg's husband made preparations for his wife's home care:

In order to organize a care-giving team for his wife, Mike Meshenberg wrote detailed guidelines for Kit's care. These guidelines included the priorities for Kit's comfort, care specific to Kit's symptoms, and instructions for drinking and eating, medication, and exercise. They were a way for Mike to manage the level of care Kit was getting even in his absence, but also a way to help friends and family know how to be a caregiver's caregivers. He also created a calendar to make sure there was someone available for Kit every day. This type of planning is important in implementing something that is by no means simple. The degree of care that is needed will shift, and watching for those shifts becomes its own task.

Seeking Help

Beyond organization and a recognition that you are doing one of the most difficult jobs in the world, the ability to seek and use help from the outside is one of the hallmarks of those who learn to cope with the size of the job.

- Know what you can do and what you cannot do. Seek outside help for those things for which you are not prepared or qualified to do.
- Know what you can control and what you cannot control. Do not blame yourself for those things that are patently out of your control.
- When help is offered, accept it.
- When you need help, go for it. Psychotherapy or counseling is not a sign of weakness; it is a sign that you recognize the strain of the work you are doing. And you *are* doing work. This thing called caregiving is a job!

Shirley Loflin's Story

Shirley Loflin, whom we met at the beginning of this chapter, did eventually find a way to deal with her burdens. Initially she cared for her husband, who suffered a stroke and was partially paralyzed and without speech. "It's tough seeing someone you love have their life completely altered and changed, and you don't have any recourse but to cope with it."

She was alone, her mother having died some years earlier, and there were no siblings. Seven years later, her father came to live with her, and there were strong demands between husband and father for her time and attention. "It's hard to be torn between a spouse and a parent," she says.

Loflin admits that she was speedily burnt out. She had had no financial responsibilities before her husband had the stroke, no experience at taking care of the checkbook, and certainly no experience prior to this in making major health, financial, and logistical decisions for ill people. Eventually she found the Carter Institute and took a course there. She realized that if she were going to survive this experience, she would have to find some respite from her chores; she would have to take some time for herself.

"I've had a lot of support from my friends. I was fortunate enough to have a good network of friends. They prodded me into taking the course, and they've helped me a lot. They didn't let me feel sorry for myself. And now I don't. I try to inject love and humor into my caregiving."

Among the many solutions to Loflin's struggles was learning for herself, then teaching financial matters to others. Asked what rewards she now enjoyed, she said something that is echoed by many: "All women, I think, feel like they need to be needed, and I definitely feel that, sometimes overwhelmingly so. I guess doing what I'm doing right now is rewarding: telling people about the help they can receive, that it's not hopeless. It's made me a better person, I think. I enjoy getting out and embracing other caregivers. No, the situation isn't hopeless. It's just changed."

Advocacy for Caregivers

We can't help adding a few words about your role as an advocate for other caregivers. After all, as a current or potential caregiver for someone in your family, wouldn't it be wonderful if someone had prepared the way, had done the groundwork that would give you and all caregivers a helping hand to make life a little less burdened? Here are some things that anyone can do to make this a reality.

- Find out about existing employee benefits at your workplace that help family caregivers, including sick leave, hospice coverage, bereavement leave, flexible spending accounts, and flexible scheduling. Work with your human resources department to add new benefits or restructure existing ones.
- Contact your senators and representatives and tell them about the valuable work of family caregivers and about their needs. Send a telegram,

make a call, or write an e-mail encouraging them to sponsor or support legislation that will improve family caregiving.

- Organize a caregiver fair at your workplace, place of worship, or local university to educate family caregivers about the resources in your community. Read about organizing a caregiver fair at www.hospicefoundation. org/care-giving/.

- Encourage caregivers you know to acknowledge and identify their strengths and challenges, to draw upon their own networks to support them, and to create a list of people on whom they can rely for specific support (e.g., those who are good listeners, good doers, respite providers).

- Help caregivers identify formal support groups, respite programs, and bereavement support by contacting groups such as local hospice programs.

11

CHILDREN AND SERIOUS ILLNESS

Children become seriously ill. Children die. Sadly, many of the deaths occur at or near birth. But many occur years later, too, when children are active and growing. Whenever serious illness occurs in children, we should give them our best care. But often we don't.

- We don't give them the right kind of pain relief.
- We don't talk to them openly enough about their illnesses or the fact that they might die.
- We don't give them options for their own care or how they wish to die.

And children mourn. Often we don't know how to help them.

- We don't talk openly with them about upcoming deaths.
- We keep them from memorial services or funerals.
- We don't let them see how much we grieve.
- When it comes to their feelings surrounding death, we often don't comprehend the intensity of that grief, or their knowledge of what's happening to them.

All of these don'ts are usually done with the best of intentions. We, the adults (whether parents or doctors), want to protect our children from bad news. We don't want them to have emotional upsets. And then there's the crucial fact that we don't, ourselves, want to admit that our children may die. So we don't talk about it. Maybe, we think, if we don't talk about it, it won't happen.

The unfortunate upshot of all of this is that children often don't receive the best medical or emotional care when they're very ill, when they're dying, or when someone else is dying.

Pain

We begin with pain because, as we pointed out in chapter 4, without proper pain management, certain illnesses are extremely difficult to bear.

It is clearly unacceptable that children should suffer from pain if there is any way to prevent it. In our society, where children are deeply valued, we should pay more attention—or at least as much attention—to their pain as to our own. The fact is, we don't. In part, as in the face of their mortality, it hurts too much to admit that our children are in pain. But a large part of our neglect results from our upbringing, current medical practice, and simple ignorance.

To begin with, many believe that children don't experience pain with the same intensity we do. We wish to believe that their tears in infancy are because they don't know how to express their feelings in words—not because it really hurts. How often parents say, in just so many words, "He's only pretending." The implication is that children really can get by without comfort for their pain and, to boot, don't really feel as we do. This has many ramifications for our care of children and, as we shall see in a few pages, significant ones for their mental health as well.

But let's stick with physical pain for now.

In July 2002, following a major Institute of Medicine report on palliative care for children, The Robert Wood Johnson Foundation held a press conference calling for a "National Blueprint" for such care. (Also issued at the time was *Last Acts: "Precepts of Palliative Care for Children."*) It pointed out that "Close to 400,000 children in the United States live annually with chronic, life-threatening conditions. Among the 53,000 each year who will die, only 10 percent will receive any palliative care, treating the whole patient—body, mind and spirit." Until now, in fact, shocking as it may seem, adults have been the primary recipients of palliative care. Sometimes it's the emotional burden that keeps parents from doing anything; sometimes it's the lack of understanding about children's pain on the part of physicians. And there are other, important factors. At the press conference, Dr. Debra Gordon laid these out:

- Depending on the age of the child or stage of development, they may or may not talk about their pain. Often they just get depressed or withdrawn, or their play may change. So someone has to be aware of changes in the play pattern as a potential manifestation of discomfort or pain.
- Other conditions such as constipation, diarrhea, and shortness of breath need to be managed. This requires people who are trained to be perceptive about the subtle signs of anxiety, for example, and the subtle physical signs of depression.
- There is the issue of what drugs to use for pain, because many are not approved for children. So we need studies of those drugs to see how they work in children. Medical school students get very little pediatric palliative care education. Some of the children's hospitals and large medical centers seem to do better in this regard. But by and large, it's still insufficient.
- Accidental injuries and sudden infant death involve people outside the health services profession. First responders are frequently firefighters and police officers, and the coroner's office is also involved. All those people are relatively uneducated about how to handle these situations and the families of the children.

Then there's the issue of *when* a child will die, and whether curative or palliative care is most appropriate. (With adults, it's easier, since they're often much older and have written advance directives.) Here's what Dr. Gordon had to say: "It's harder to predict the end of life in children for a variety of reasons related to their biology. So if you have a child with a serious cancer, at the same time you want to make sure palliative and end-of-life plans are being made, while acknowledging the possibility of survival. Curative and palliative treatments go hand in hand. For example, you might want to make sure the child gets immunized against pneumococcal infections at the same time you're continuing with some anti-cancer drugs."

All of these factors play into the diminished care given to children's emotional and physical pain. But the fact is, as Dr. Joanne Hilden (chair of the pediatric department of oncology at the Cleveland Hospital) said, "People don't want to hear about dying, they want to hear about curing. What we see in the trenches every day is that we need to help parents to hope for the best, yet plan for the worst, just in case. We find we have little opportunities here and there to plant the notion that there is help, that we can prevent suffering and let death be peaceful, should it happen."

There, in a nutshell, are two of the big challenges: to get parents to recognize the need for palliative care, and to provide for such care in the medical system.

In fact, the latter may be a bigger challenge, since right now very few pediatric palliative specialists exist. Taking care of children's bodies and children's health is already a specialty for which training is necessary, but beyond that, the use of painkillers and other palliative measures for children has just not been carefully studied or taught. Not to mention that the present HMO system, with its short discussions and short office visits the norm, is not helpful when trying to educate frightened parents about a new kind of care for their child.

The Way Things Could Be

It might help to relate the story of one child who was dying and did receive the care of a palliative pediatric specialist.

Jennifer Phelan's only child, Georgiana, was diagnosed with lymphoma, a cancer of the blood. "When she relapsed, I knew she wouldn't make it. I didn't want to feel that way, but I did. I didn't tell anybody that, because I was afraid I would get yelled at, having to say something like that or feel something like that, so I did whatever (my doctor) wanted to do as far as the chemo(therapy)." When the disease failed to respond, her primary care oncologist mentioned pediatric palliative care as an option. What Phelan and her daughter would experience for the next two months is a quietly growing medical specialty that includes the smallest dying patients and their families in critical medical decisions. Teams of specialists worked together to tend to the emotional, psychological, practical, and spiritual needs of the patient and family. Child life specialists, psychologists, hospice professionals, social workers, and spiritual counselors were called in to help the family say their good-byes and prepare for what lay ahead.

Once Georgiana was admitted, her hospital room immediately was transformed into a homelike setting. Her parents brought her teddy bear and baby blanket, which she had slept with every night since she was born. "I think it was important that Georgiana had a child psychologist talk to her and I think she helped her a whole lot." As Georgiana's condition worsened, her doctor and the palliative care team discussed the family's options, including if, when, and how to let her die naturally: stopping the antibiotics; no more trips to the intensive care unit. Whether to set up hospice care at home. Saying no to life-support systems. And planning for a funeral.

"The hardest decision was stopping those antibiotics, but I knew I didn't want Georgie on life support. I mean, I don't think I could've seen her like that." As death neared, managing Georgiana's pain with morphine became everyone's number-one priority.

So what you as a parent of a really ill child can do is:

- Ask in your community about pediatric palliative care specialists.
- Be aware that your child has pain, just like you do, and ask about it. If the child can't tell you, don't assume there is no pain. Get professional help to assess pain and address it.
- Recognize your own denial about the seriousness of your child's illness or, if you're emotionally too distraught to deal with it, get another adult (relative or not) as well as a psychological counselor to help with your child's care.

Last Acts Partnership suggests we acknowledge that children (and their families) deserve special attention when it comes to palliative care, as follows:

- Identify and honor the preferences of the child or adolescent as to values, goals, and priorities as well as cultural and spiritual perspectives.
- Assist the child, adolescent, and family in establishing goals of care by facilitating their understanding of the diagnosis and prognosis.
- Place a high priority on physical comfort and functional capacity, including, but not limited to, expert management of pain and other symptoms, diagnosis and treatment of psychological distress, and assistance in remaining as independent as possible or desired.
- Provide physical, psychological, social and spiritual support to help the child or adolescent and the family adapt to the anticipated decline associated with advanced, progressive, incurable disease.

- Extend support beyond the life span of the child to assist the family in their bereavement through ongoing support, guidance, and remembrance.
- Anticipate that some family caregivers may be at high risk for fatigue, physical illness, and emotional distress and consider the special needs of these caregivers in planning and delivering services.
- Finally, and very importantly, recognize the economic costs of caregiving, including loss of income and nonreimbursable expenses.

What Your Child Already Knows

One of the clear differences between thinking about adults and children is that parents—and physicians—very often ignore the fact that children know that they're dying, and that they have wishes of their own as to how to die. Children as young as six or seven are acutely aware of the fact that they are seriously ill and will even know when it is time to "let go." Team members caring for dying children frequently recognize the depth of their patients' perception and awareness.

For instance, picking up on our previous story, unlike her parents, Georgiana quickly came to terms with her condition. Phelan describes it simply: "Mommy sees the doctor. Mommy leaves the room. Mommy comes back in crying. You can't hide it from them. They're going to figure it out on their own. Her fear was leaving us. She had said to me, 'If I die, I won't see you anymore.' And I told her she would, because she could watch us from heaven. And then she didn't talk about it again. She said that every night when I go to sleep, she'll come into my room and give me a kiss," Phelan said.

As Georgiana got sicker, her mother recalls her asking, "Mom, am I going to die?" "And I couldn't answer her. I said, 'I don't know.' I said, 'That's what we're all afraid of because the medicine didn't work.' And she cried. And that was it—she stopped and went to do whatever she was doing."

While the ability of children to know about their own mortality and to come to terms with it seems almost unbelievable, it is crucial that parents recognize that children cannot be fooled, and that acknowledging that death is near can offer an opportunity to help the entire family grieve before and after death. It is a remarkable experience when it is done as close to "right" as it can be.

Liza's Story

Here is another family that seems to have done it right. While this is a long excerpt from a published book, it is, we believe, worth taking the time to read it—and for us to print it. It shows that even very young children can be aware of their own mortality, that they can prepare for their own deaths—and that in so doing they may make life easier for parent and child alike. This is from *Giving Voice to Sorrow: Personal Responses to Death and Mourning* by Steve Zeitlin and Ilana Harlow (Penguin Putnam, 2001). It's the story of Liza Lister, who was diagnosed with leukemia before she was four and lived only two more years. Her parents were apparently very aware of how smart and aware Liza was, and they talked with her openly about her illness. It paid off.

When Liza was admitted into the hospital for pain control, we knew there was nothing else they could offer her. We were awaiting the biopsy results. Both Phil and myself always knew when it was going to be bad news. Before the diagnosis came, we knew. So we had this feeling that it was going to be our worst fear. And her bone marrow transplant doctor came into her room and told her that the leukemia was back. And I was surprised Lizie didn't ask anything at that point. She nodded. I saw that she took it in.

It was my turn to stay with her in the hospital that night. Phil and I took turns. We always watched a lot of Nickelodeon in the evening and I think probably we had rented a movie. And then we were getting ready for bed and were in the bathroom, and she was brushing her teeth and doing a last potty stop. I think I actually was kneeling down next to her helping her with her clothes because her skin was very sensitive.

And that's when she said, "Am I always going to have my leukemia?"
I remember thinking, "Okay, here we go."
She must have been sitting and working though this that afternoon.
I said, "Yeah, we think so."
Then she said, "Am I gonna die from my leukemia?"
I said, "Yeah, we think so."
And then she said, "Am I gonna die soon?"
And I said, "We don't know when."
She said, "Well, will I get to be a teenager?"

I said, "I don't think so."

"Will I get to be a Mommy?"

"I don't think so."

That broke my heart because she would have been a great mom.

At each of these questions I said, "I don't think so." At that point I was down on my knees. We were eye to eye and she was leaning on my shoulder and I was holding her, chest to chest. She paused for a minute and tried to take it all in. And then she said, "I know how I want to die." It just totally blew me away. My guess is that she'd thought about it before, actually. We'd had one or two other conversations about dying, but I think she must have been doing a lot more thinking than she told us about.

"I want to die on your lap. I want to have my lullaby tape on." Then she said, "I want you to die with me." I remember thinking at the time, "I think I will." I could tell she was really picturing this scene because she immediately said, "No, no, no, no. I want you to die right *after* me. I want you to die right after me so you can be with me when I die."

So she really was imagining the scene. She wanted me to be intact, able to be a giving presence while she actually died; then I'd follow her. When she was four and a half she said she didn't want to die because she didn't want to be alone. And, I mean, who does? It's the ultimate aloneness. So I think that was just in keeping with the same line of thinking. So she set a stage. Later on there were elaborations: "I want to die at home. What will dying be like? How will I know when I'm actually dying?"

That night, after our conversation in the bathroom, she wanted to sleep on me. And I remember feeling her heart beating against me, and feeling like, "I want to make this moment indelibly imprinted on my mind because I'm not going to have this." Her back was to my chest, and I have a vague recollection of a conversation. Lights out in the room, her lying on me and her saying, "So will you die with me?"

That was Liza. I think other kids might have just let it go. And I don't think I ever said "no." I said, "A part of me is going to die with you, and a part of you is going to stay alive with me for always and forever."

We had an oncologist who was not comfortable facing Liza's terminal condition with her and did not understand that Liza was a "need to know" kind of person. Although we had told Liza that she was dying, he continued to speak to her as though she were not necessarily terminal. The mixed messages made her anxious. We scheduled a meeting with him so she could ask him questions. We listened as she narrowed her window of remaining life to a smaller and smaller future. "Will I get to be seven? Will I live to be six?" We didn't prompt these questions. They were totally from her.

And he looked like, "Oh my God. I can't believe I have to answer this," and then answered her. He told her that she would not live until her seventh birthday and that he hoped she would live until her sixth. He told her that we would know when the day was soon and that he would tell her when her time was near. That conversation was reassuring for Liza. She knew the truth, she knew that we knew it, and she needed to know that we could all know it together. After that talk Liza grew less anxious. When she asked the oncologist, "Will I live to my sixth birthday? "and he said "I hope so," that became her goal: to get to be six.

In fact, Liza did live until she was six—just barely. And, according to her mother's account, she was able to think about her death in many of the ways we wish we could: when the time came to let go, she let go.

Children Mourn

Adding to a child's shock and confusion at the death of a brother, sister, or parent is the unavailability of other family members, who may be so shaken by grief that they are not able to cope with the normal responsibility of child care.
—American Academy of Child and Adolescent Psychiatry

It often happens that adults and children share the same *experiences*, but don't exhibit the same *behavior*. It is the adult who seems to show the most emotion at a death, so it is the adult we think about and care for. The child often suffers silently—or in ways we don't understand—and so we often find it difficult to determine when a child is feeling the worst, and how to assuage that suffering.

Everyone knows situations where there was a death in the family and the children were ignored during the dying process. A parent may have thought, "My child doesn't really understand what's happening, so why upset them?" Or even, "They'd be too frightened to say good-bye to their father, so don't tell them about the funeral."

Yes, some children may be too frightened or angry to go to a funeral or memorial ceremony, but specialists in child psychology suggest that all children should be encouraged to remember their father or grandmother or friend in any way they choose: a scrapbook, telling stories, and sharing photographs are good ideas.

Sometimes children express their feelings of dismay or bewilderment or loss in anger, often at inappropriate times, and over a much longer time span than we expect—or would like! Adults can get very upset at a sudden unexplained burst of anger in the middle of dinner.

But precisely at the time when the child needs to be told that his mourning or anger is justified, we tend to be upset by it and try to stop it. It may remind us that we, too, are losing a loved one, or it may just be an irritation that we cannot shake off.

But, rather than reprimanding the child, we should try to respect her feelings and spend time in reassurance: "The world will go on. Life will go on. You will survive." The child needs to be told that.

One of the wonderful things about recognizing and acknowledging children's abilities to deal with sorrow is the burden it lifts from adults. Sometime back we listened to a tape from a radio station in upstate New York, WUWM. It had participated in a Benton Foundation project dealing with death and dying, and decided to do a few programs on children's reactions. It was absolutely fascinating.

The reporter, Tracy Fields, started out, "Sooner or later, every kid will have a personal encounter with death. When that happens, adults often try to shield children, but these protective efforts can easily backfire. Life lessons can be squandered by fears of adults."

The program went on to spell out some of the key things we should and should not do.

- We should not lie to our children about the finality of death, and should recognize that, given the facts, they can often handle it better than we.
- Children should be allowed to attend funerals or memorial services if

they wish to. Mourning in public can be a wonderful way for them to deal with the crisis. Denial is not.

- Since dealing with grief is a life skill, let children see you cry. It won't hurt you, and it won't hurt them. Explain what's going on, that you miss the dead person, and that it's okay to be sad. And if the child can't deal with that sadness then, they'll let you know. Don't force the issue.
- Recognize that different children at different ages will react to or deal with illness or death in a different fashion. If something doesn't resonate with them today, it very well may tomorrow. And if we allow children to deal with these things over a period of time, but honestly, we allow them to grow.
- Finally, the program suggested that parents be aware that things can be scary around the house for a while after a death. Leaving a light on or letting a child stay part of the night in a parent's room can be a simple way of dealing with that.

Here are some words of wisdom from a book published by the American Hospice Foundation, *Living with Grief: Children, Adolescents, and Loss* (www.hospicefoundation.org).

Sarah, after the death of a close teen-age friend: I had never faced anything like this and had no idea how to handle it emotionally. Talking about what happened, seeking comfort in those who were having similar feelings as me, and talking about Tammi were what helped me through my disbelief and my struggle to figure out a reason behind it all. I still have not figured out why this happened, but I do know I learned a lot about myself and about true friends in those days, lessons that could not have come any other way. I think what helped me when I returned to school was having those friends willing to listen to my stories and to share in memories.

Maggie (thirteen years old): To me, it's impossible to tell someone how to grieve. You can help someone, but never instruct them. I've been to a few grief camps and groups for the loss of my brother Gary and my grandfather Robert. At both, they showed us movies or diagrams about the grieving process. I never really understood them. To me, everyone grieves in a different way, and you shouldn't analyze that, or tell them how it works. Certain things were not helpful . . . people would ask, "How's your brother, Maggie?" But they seemed to forget about me. I was still there! Another annoying thing that people did, mainly my friends, was to try to cheer me up when I felt sad, try to make me laugh and forget about it. It was well intentioned, but I wanted to cry. I needed to cry. I couldn't forget. I wanted to talk about it, not to laugh at something. My advice to anyone talking to a person in mourning is to be kind, gentle, and a constant support. Offer to talk, but do not pressure them. They will trust you and if they need to talk, they seek you out.

Guilt

If we don't talk to children about the death, they can easily imagine that it is their fault, and that's why no one is talking to them. Young children, who often engage in what is called "magical thinking," may feel that they are responsible for illness and death. Perhaps they got angry at Grandma, and she took ill the next week. This is the same irrational guilt that makes children feel that they have caused a divorce or a parental argument, and that they have to find some way to make everything okay again. They don't consciously blame themselves, and most don't share what they're feeling with an adult. But it can be extremely helpful for the parent or other adult to find a way to reassure the child that the death of a loved one is *not* his or her fault; that no matter how often the child was angry at the parent or thought "bad thoughts," these could never have an effect on the parent's health.

So, summing up, here are some of the things parents can do to make children who are grieving more comfortable.

Spend time with your children; help them with their grief. You'll get help with yours, too.

Make sure children are allowed to express their feelings. It may be uncomfortable to hear them shout or swear or say strange things, but it is their way of reacting to a truly traumatic experience in their life. Yes, we know, you didn't do anything wrong and it's unsettling to have your child yell at you, but accept it for what it is: anger at the loss of a person important to your child.

Do not be surprised if the anger or other reactions last over a long time, or surface a few weeks or months later. Who said kids had perfect timing?

Keep an eye out for effects that last too long. Be aware that for some children the loss may be too great. According to the American Academy of Child and Adolescent Psychiatry, "Children who are having serious problems with grief and loss may show one or more of these signs:

- An extended period of depression in which the child loses interest in daily activities and events
- Inability to sleep, loss of appetite, prolonged fear of being alone
- Acting much younger for an extended period
- Excessively imitating the dead person
- Repeated statements of wanting to join the dead person
- Withdrawal from friends, or
- Sharp drop in school performance or refusal to attend school

If these signs do show up, *adults should seek the help of a professional therapist or psychiatrist for their child."*

An important study in New York, carried out by Grace Christ, Ph.D. and her colleagues at the Columbia University School of Social Work, looked at children's grief. The study reported that children can recover relatively quickly from grief *if:*

1. They are given attention *during* a loved one's illness, not just afterward. Dr. Christ says they need to be prepared for the impending death and the strength of their feelings.
2. There are not too many other stressors in their lives (such as alcoholism or poverty).
3. We recognize that children in our culture often won't express their grief publicly, so that feelings may be hidden, but those feelings are nonetheless strong.

Children as Caregivers

In our last chapter we dealt with the stresses of caregiving. We want to mention briefly the unfortunate fact that sometimes children become surrogate caregivers, with all the attendant stress that that entails.

This may come about informally or by accident, as when a parent or other adult (such as a doctor) tries to keep the house quiet for an ill relative. At times like these, the child is seen as an impediment to good medical care, or to the peace and quiet of the adults who are worried about the patient. Interested in being a "good child," these children can take on the "quietly suffering" role of a caregiver, doing everything they can to help their parents, the doctors, and the ill person, ignoring their own needs. They often remain more silent and less openly upset than do adults. As always, children need to be reminded that they neither caused the illness nor made it worse.

The second case is where children are actually required to be active caregivers. This can happen when a younger child falls ill. It can also happen when financial need requires that adults leave the home to work or to get medicine, and leave the young child in charge of the house and the ill person. This is not the role we might wish for our children, but all too often necessity makes them take on adult jobs. The result is not healthy, and when at all possible, children should *not* be made to take the caregiver role. One needs to remember that even the littlest caregiver feels stress and needs attention paid.

Storytelling and Laughter

We want to end this chapter with special reference to two ways of comforting children, whether they are seriously ill or are mourning someone else's death; ways that are terribly easy and in our repertory, things we can easily forget when the stress of serious illness is upon us, or the house is settled in mourning.

Giving Comfort

Telling children stories or reading to them has a remarkably comforting effect. When we are very young it is one of the ways our parents sit with us when we are going to sleep; it is something we do when a child has a cold; it is something we do when they are frightened and come knocking on our door in the middle of the night.

It doesn't matter, then, whether you tell them a story about your family (our kids love to hear about a long-gone grandmother or grandfather), or read them a childhood favorite, or—like one mother we know—make up a story that has a little moral to it, a comforting tale of grief coming to an end.

Any kind of storytelling can take a child away from the pain and fear and into a land of make-believe. Eyes glaze over, not in discomfort, but in dreaming about a different time, a different kind of world. The BBC radio service used to offer just such a storytelling hour for young children at two in the afternoon every day. "Now, young ones," it began, "climb into your mummy's lap and get comfortable." This introduction was followed by the most wonderful series of stories.

So for those children who are up in the middle of the night with sadness or fear or physical pain, keep in mind the power of the story.

Laughter

We brought this up in chapter 4, but we want to do so again in this context.

Here's what is happening at the University of California at Los Angeles Jonsson Cancer Center, a formidable research institute. They are well into a five-year, carefully controlled investigative study on whether laughter can actually help a child's immune system to resist serious diseases.

It's already known that humor can alleviate stress and fear, which inhibit some kinds of healing, but can laughter actually *cure?*

To find out, here's what UCLA researchers did:

First, they found out what made kids laugh.

Second, they showed videos that had been proven to make healthy children laugh to those with AIDS or cancer.

Third, they investigated whether the laughter *by itself* can improve the immune system and lead to quick or better recovery from serious disease. As of this writing, the study is still going on; answers are not yet forthcoming.

But if— "If, indeed, laughter and good humor do prompt positive physiologic responses, [the investigators] hope to integrate them into treatment procedures for young patients. For example, children and adolescents undergoing chemotherapy or other frightening procedures could be shown humorous programming to help alleviate stress and fear, which can inhibit healing. Such integration of conventional medicine and laughter would represent change in the way medicine is practiced at UCLA."

Suppose it were true that laughter could in fact cure; that would be wonderful. But we already know that it's good for children. We watch them laugh and know they are truly in less pain while they're laughing. "We already have a pretty good idea about the impact that laughter and humor can have on a person's mental well-being," say the UCLA doctors.

So, why wait? Why not use humor as a way of

- Comforting children
- Distracting them from pain
- Bringing caregiver and child closer together in a pleasant fashion
- Giving children something to do (other than fear) when undergoing blood tests or chemotherapy?

In fact, we can think of lots of ways in which humor can be used when children are ill or dying. Your child may not think that he or she can laugh while undergoing treatment or fearing the doctor's next visit. Try it. You may be surprised.

12

NURSING HOMES

As we have said throughout this book, most Americans want to die at home, but only 10 percent get to do so. Over half die in hospitals, and as many as 25 percent die in nursing homes. The nursing home population is something over 1.8 million. That means that in any one year, approximately 400,000 people die in nursing homes.

Yet nursing homes are the one place most people say they definitely want to stay away from if they're seriously ill or dying. Why? Nursing homes have gotten a bad reputation over the last three decades. There have been scandals involving corruption. There have been investigations about lack of care, and the wrong kind of care.

In fact, many people continue to think of the wards and rooms of nursing homes as foul-smelling, full of bedridden patients restrained by belts or creeping slowly along the hallways in wheelchairs. The image of overcrowded nursing homes is not much different from the image of mental hospitals around the 1940s: a place to warehouse dying people.

There are other, perhaps more important reasons why people don't want to use nursing homes, prominent among them the desire to stay in familiar and comfortable surroundings when we're ill. We don't want to leave behind the companions and loved ones who have, up to now, been able to interpret and satisfy many of our emotional and physical needs.

It is important, then, to consider the facts about nursing homes, as compared to the myths about them. Most of the following comes from the federally funded Centers for Disease Control:

- While a few nursing homes continue to use physical and chemical restraints on residents, federal laws and state watchdogs, plus education, have eliminated most of such usage, to the benefit not only of the residents, but the nursing homes as well. It turns out, for instance, that restraints can contribute to fall-related injuries and deaths, partly because limiting a patient's freedom of movement leads to muscle weakness and reduces physical function. Since 1990, when new laws went into effect, there have been, for the most part, fewer falls, fewer serious injuries, and fewer lawsuits.
- In 1997, over one-half of elderly nursing home residents were eighty-five years of age or older.
- Nursing home residents are predominantly white women. The most common reasons for admission were circulatory diseases and cognitive and mental disorders.
- A growing number of residents are entering homes because they require assistance with activities of daily living (ADLs) such as bathing, dressing, and eating, and, additionally, because they could not write checks, use the phone, do simple shopping, and the like.

And here's an interesting fact: people are staying a *shorter* time in nursing homes these days, not because they die, but often because of an increase in the use of home health care *and* an increase in patients who have "moved from short-stay hospitals to nursing homes for rehabilitation and then are discharged back to the community." Improvements in medical care, healthy living, visiting nurses, hospice, better insurance—all go toward helping old people stay in the home, where, for the most part, quality of life is better than in an institution.

Looking into the future, the CDC estimates that by 2030, there may be as many as 3 million residents of nursing homes (more than a 50% increase) *unless* home care increases tremendously.

Which means that unless we want to be blind to the facts, it is best to push for changes in nursing home financing and quality of life while also increasing the amount of home care that is available.

It's also important to recognize that no matter how good home care is, the so-called "informal caregivers" (wives, daughters, husbands, children) cannot possibly sustain the twenty-four-hour care that is needed for seriously ill people. Even when hospice is added for the terminally ill, there are times when even the best-intentioned and trained caregiver gives up. For instance, when cognitive impairment becomes moderate or severe, behaviors such as hitting, wandering, or being unable to keep oneself out of danger can become too much for a caregiver to manage.

How Nursing Home Care Falls Short

But let's look at some of the negative facts stated by federal watchdogs and other observers.

- Most nursing homes do not have an affiliated hospice.
- The record of palliative care measures in nursing homes is dismal. According to a remarkable series of audiotapes (Heart to Heart: Improving Care for the Dying Through Public Policy, obtainable from Last Acts Partnership), "Many states count somebody dying in a nursing home as a negative quality indicator. So the nursing home may want to get that person out of the nursing home before they die. They put the person in the ambulance, the ambulance takes them to the emergency room. So they will be trying to resuscitate you and they will be putting tubes in your throat, and they'll be pounding on your chest and they will be starting IV's and putting catheters in your bladder. You'll be started on a breathing machine. Sometimes you need to be heavily sedated so that you don't fight the breathing machine. And if you had a living will or an advanced directive, chances are that hospital won't know it. So, it can end up being a nightmare for the patient and the family."

Pain management isn't much better. In fact, according to a report by The Robert Wood Johnson Foundation and Last Acts, nursing homes are generally miserable at taking care of residents' pain, which may often be left untreated. A national study conducted in 1999 found that nearly one-sixth of nursing home patients are in daily pain, and more than 40 percent of residents who were in pain at their first pain assessment were still in severe pain 60 to 180 days later. Another recent study found that many dying nursing home residents who are in daily pain receive either inadequate pain treatment or none at all. "These findings are sobering, given that many nursing home residents have chronic conditions, and more than 20 percent of residents die there—a figure projected to double by 2020. Adequate pain management for seriously ill and dying nursing home residents is essential to achieving high quality end-of-life care."

One year ago, Robert Wagner, eighty-one, moved to a nursing home after a stroke impaired his speech and paralyzed his right side. Robert found it awkward and embarrassing to communicate. He struggled to complete a sentence and was ashamed to gesture because of his immobilized right arm. He seemed to avoid talking, even when his wife and friends were there. Whenever nurses and physicians asked him how he felt, he routinely answered, "Fine."

One day, Robert's occupational therapist noticed that he was frowning and blinking often. Although he said, as usual, that he was fine, the therapist consulted with a physician, who referred him to an ophthalmologist. During the eye exam, the ophthalmologist inadvertently leaned against Robert's left leg. Robert let out a cry, and tears welled up in his eyes. The ophthalmologist then realized that Robert was in pain. Further testing revealed a cancer in his right femur.

Robert's pain would not have gone unnoticed if the staff in his nursing home had been properly trained to identify pain in their patients, even in those who cannot communicate. Providers qualified to prescribe medications are experienced in selecting the right pain medication at the right dosage, and nursing home staff should have checked Robert's comfort level frequently, knowing that pain can flare up unpredictably. (Adapted from www.partnersagainstpain.org by permission.)

Further, researchers at the University of Pittsburgh surveyed nursing home residents who experienced pain on a daily basis, and found that many do not mention their pain to staff. Residents' reasons for not doing so include fear that they may become addicted to pain medication, belief that pain is untreatable, and belief that staff will not answer their complaints.

Interestingly enough, nursing homes that want to improve their performance with regard to pain can find help in doing so from quality improvement organizations based in each state and under contract with Medicare. According to The Robert Wood Johnson Foundation report, this can make a difference. For instance, in Colorado, about 50 of 225 facilities sought help from the quality improvement organizations, officials there said. At Clear Creek Care Center in Westminster, Colorado, a team of six nursing home employees attended a half-day workshop once a month with improvement experts. There they were taught what they could do to better identify and care for residents in pain. The result was that the number of Clear Creek residents who reported experiencing pain dropped radically, officials said. "We can really say now in our facility that all staff is aware of our philosophy about pain," nursing home administrator Beth Irtz said.

Whatever the good—and bad—trends in nursing homes, whatever the good—or bad—news, most people do not want to spend their last months or days in them. This results only partly from what we read in the news or hear on television. It also results from visits to nursing homes, where the sight of bedridden or wheelchair-bound people whose daily functioning is drastically reduced and the smell of urine or disinfectant tends to turn us away in fear or dismay. This is not surprising. While residents can get used to the atmosphere of a nursing home, only the greatest attention to décor, hygiene, and care can make most visitors feel that such institutions are a good place for their loved ones.

In short, nursing homes remind us of what we have been struggling to escape at any cost: death as a painful, lonely, frightening, and messy experience. You may read all this and wonder why those who advocate for quality care at the end of life don't focus more energy on reducing the number of people who die in institutions by bringing long-term care into the home, or by providing hospice care in hospitals or at home. The answer is complicated, but in its simplest form it boils down to the fact that millions of Americans either do not have the money or insurance to have care at home for their loved ones, or cannot provide the amount of personal caregiving that is required at home (even with hospice or other support), or simply do not have the psychological wherewithal to take care of a dying relative in their home.

In addition, sadly, millions of Americans may not have a living relative who wants to take care of them, or is available to do so.

So, for the near term at least, the nursing home must be considered a place where Americans will continue to spend time when chronically or terminally ill, and where they will eventually die. Even though more residents are being released from homes to return to their families, and the ability to cure or remediate illness is improving, nonetheless, long-term care facilities will remain a place where millions will die.

Improving Institutional Care

The best thing to do, then, is to find some way of making such facilities better places to receive care. This, of course, is what the federal government has been doing with its emphasis on reduction of the use of restraints, and with its more recent attention to a wide variety of details of nursing home care in America's institutions.

Here are a couple of very important ways for *you* to check up on the suitability of a local nursing home.

• Visit Medicare's Website (www.medicare.gov) and access *Nursing Home Compare,* a database with information about every Medicare/Medicaid-certified nursing home in the country, organized by state, county, and city. (You can go there directly at www.medicare.gov/Nursing/Overview. asp, but the general Medicare site also offers other rich information.) There, families will get information on ten quality indicators examining such things as the prevalence of physical restraints at a facility and the percentage of residents who have bed sores. Information on deficiencies found during annual inspections and complaint investigations also is being made available.
• Read *Your Guide to Choosing a Nursing Home,* a booklet available from the Health Care Financing Administration of the U.S. Department of Health and Human Services:
7500 Security Boulevard
Baltimore, MD 21244
1-800-633-4227
www.medicare.gov/Publications/Pubs/pdf/nhguide.pdf
　　All of the information is based on data that nursing homes must routinely collect from the home's residents as part of their participation in the federal Medicare program. In addition to providing consumers useful information, government officials are hoping that the new availability of information will prompt facilities to make improvements.
• Contact your long-term care ombudsmen's office. There's one in each state. Call them and ask questions about the nursing home that interests you.

And, of course, it is also necessary to visit any nursing home you wish to utilize and to make decisions based on considerations other than those in the Medicare database, to report untoward conditions or treatment, and to keep your options open.

It is also wise to continue to push within your community for changes in the reimbursement systems: not only for home care through Medicare and for lower-cost long-term care insurance that might permit us to have our loved ones at home, but for the reimbursement of hospice care in all nursing homes.

While we continue to utilize nursing homes, to help them improve, the ultimate goal in our view is to permit as many people as possible to live the last years of their lives where they want to live; to die where they want to die—and for most of us that is in familiar surroundings with our loved ones, and with the utmost in palliative care, all reimbursed by a beneficent tax base!

13

WHEN CRISES COME

W hen sorrows come," says King Claudius in *Hamlet,* "they come not single spies, but in battalions."

And so it often seems, when we are struck by illness, whether that of a loved one or that of our own.

But, in fact, the perception of a crisis *as a crisis* is intermittent. The human psyche is remarkable in its ability to pass through a difficult time and move on to the good ones. And with most of the serious diseases or illnesses that can strike us, we find that there are low points of pain and fear, and plateaus of ordinary living.

Still, crises do come, and we need to talk about them, for that is where preparedness is a blessing and where, through fear or dismay or forgetfulness or lack of preparation, we sometimes leave out things we can do to help ourselves or those we love at the time, and for years to come.

What we talk about in this chapter can be frightening, but it can also be terribly reassuring. There *are* things to do when crises come that can make us steady in our determination not to let things get out of control, no matter how fearful and threatening they may be—or appear to be.

The Diagnosis

Learning that you have a serious illness is the first blow: it is the kind of news that would shake anyone, the news that says, "You are mortal, and we're here to make sure you know that!" No matter what our age, when we are told that we have cancer (or ALS or MS or any serious disease), the news is bound to shake us—unless we are that rare breed of individual who can walk on coals of fire and not flinch. Even with all the best thinking ahead, the best preparation, this is scary.

Lukas's Story _____

"How are you?" my physician asked, over the phone.

"Fine," I said, totally not expecting what was to follow.

"I'm afraid I have some bad news for you."

I sank into my chair, knowing what was coming, knowing that doctors and hospitals can't be trusted, knowing that if there was a chance of something bad happening, it would.

It was four months after the biopsy had come back "clean," two months after my fifty-seventh birthday. A small lump on my neck, originally thought to be a benign, unimportant lesion, was now definitely lymphoma.

_____

It is at this point that you must muster all your resources. If you have made preparations ahead of time—living wills, health care agents, conversations about end-of-life wishes, investigations of palliative care—then you are garrisoned against some of the fear. If you have not made such preparations, now is the time to make them. Even though we prefer that you prepare in advance, what's called "just-in-time action" can be very powerful.

One of the first things to do, of course, is to make sure you heard right, or, perhaps, to get a second opinion. Did you just get a death notice from your physician, or is there another way of looking at the situation? It's here, during this initial diagnosis crisis, that one can learn just how badly communication can be carried on, despite everyone's attempt to "get it right."

Lukas's Story _____

When my wife and I went to see the oncologist, Dr. M., who would become one of my closest allies over the next decade, we got a thorough briefing on this disease known as lymphoma. When we showed up for our appointment, we were both in terrible shape. Despite a gene for gallows humor, we were not in good spirits. Human vulnerability had struck us. Dr. M. started off with my physical history. I told him everything I knew, both about myself and my relatives. Then he told me everything he thought I should know about the disease, starting with the difference between benign lymph nodes and follicular hyperplastic non-Hodgkin's lymphoma (malignant ones). Of the non-Hodgkins variety, there are sixteen different lymphomas. Some are "low-grade," some medium, some high. The best kind to have—if you have to have any—are the low kind: slow-moving, doubling in size only every six months or so. "Yours is low grade," he said, and there was a slightly perceptible lifting of the weight that had been pressing against my bowels. Then there are the "stages." "Staging," Dr. M. went on, means that the investigators need to find out in how many places (abdomen, bone marrow, armpits, groin) the lymphoma has begun to appear. "We don't know yours yet." Stage I—just one node discovered—would be terrific. It might require treatment, but would deliver a good prognosis for survival. He went on: lymphoma is a *chronic* disease. It's noncurable, and requires monitoring and treatment for one's entire life.

"Median survival rates for your kind of lymphoma are between seven and ten years from discovery of the disease."

I know Dr. M. thought he was reassuring me with his "chronic" instead of "acute," his seven-to-ten-year survival rate, his stages, and his battery of tests. But, in fact, I was not enjoying our discussion nor, as it turned out later, listening as carefully as I should have. I kept thinking about the fact that I did not have enough health insurance; that, given the strenuous nature of my job, I might not be able to continue it if the disease got out of control. I thought of the trips I'd planned to make in my old age, of the college payments still owed, of my younger daughter's wish to go to law school. Of how we had always struggled to make all our payments on time, to keep out of debt, but how we owed $40,000 on a home equity loan.

Most of all, I didn't want to be sick. I wanted to go on living until a stroke took me down—cleanly, without warning—at age eighty-five or so.

In chapter 6, and elsewhere, we have stressed communication with your physicians. But when you're frightened, it's very difficult to be clearheaded about what they say, or to think about asking the right questions. In fact, it may not be until much later that you get it straight. That's why it's good to have partners in your thinking about this.

And to give yourself a break. Of course, this is frightening. *But it may not be as serious as you think.* In fact, this may be a scary beginning to a long-term but not terminal illness. In fact, millions of us face this kind of crisis all the time. As medical prowess gets better and better, the crisis of a bad diagnosis becomes more and more routine and, for millions, turns into standard tests and treatments, not to mention wonderful things called *remediation* and *respite,* not imminent death.

Treatment

However, the first days of testing and treatment can also be crises. Hospitals are frightening places, the jargon of medical personnel can be off-putting, and the fear of serious illness and death can hang over the entire process.

Lukas's Story _____

The CT scan. Arrived early at the hospital. They kept me waiting for ten minutes, then told me I was in the wrong wing. Amazing how the smallest thing can make me feel put upon and lost. Still, they're remarkably nice people, facing disaster and death as they do every day. Found the proper waiting room, sat down, was told to drink three huge paper cups filled with Tang tinged with iodine. A young resident physician officially warns me that the intravenous iodine shot I was about to get might cause heart palpitations or allergic reactions, and then asked me to sign a release. Another doctor asked me to step into her cubicle so she could put in my intravenous needle. First try, the needle went through my vein and out the other side. Oops. She said she'd prefer a vein in my hand. I'm sitting there, covering my eyes, afraid of needles since birth, glad I took a Xanax for my nerves. Then, suddenly, I'm up on the table, being measured for the proper distance from the scanner. The iodine drip begins, and I feel a warm rush to my head. The scan takes only twenty minutes, a scientific marvel, this series of X-rays that slices my body into cross-sections, highlighted by the iodine "blocker," so that bowel can be distinguished from alien lumps, veins from lymph nodes, lungs from hyperplastic invaders. (Later I will begin to understand how my fascination with the technical hides my terror.)

But it doesn't take long, even with the most awful words hanging over our heads ("lesion," "median survival rates," "PET scans, biopsies, bone marrow transplant") to get used to the process, to accommodate ourselves to the idea that we are not going to die for a long time to come. In the months and years ahead, we find that it's even possible to slip into the hospital for a checkup, get it done, and go back to normal living within a few minutes.

Recurrence

After a period of remission, it's easy to fall into the state of a regular patient, to assume that our days of crisis are over. Then comes a recurrence or, as in the case of Lukas, a second kind of cancer.

Lukas's Story

It was eight years after my lymphoma had become a livable, chronic disease that I was diagnosed with prostate cancer. It was still startling. It was still frightening. But it was not a crisis. By now, I had made my living will. I had appointed my wife to be my agent. I had thought a lot about palliative care, about hospice, about chronic versus. terminal illnesses. When I went in for my forty days of radiation, I had already undergone my lymphoma radiation; I had already known what it was like to live with cancer and yearly checkups and CT scans. In short, I was no longer a virgin in this business of serious disease.

Was I still worried? Of course. Was I still angry at the insult of being hit a second time? For sure! But it was no longer the kind of threat the first cancer had been. I was learning to live with dying.

Surgery

No matter how prepared you are, no matter how many times crises have come and gone, when you have to go into the hospital for an operation or for more serious kinds of treatment, the negative emotions begin all over again.

Again, you can't get your head screwed on straight.

Again, you mis-hear things.

Again, you and your family are thrown into panic.

It takes every bit of strength you have to calm yourself.

So, here are some hints for you and your family when this happens:

- Don't be afraid to ask for a tranquilizer. That's what they're for!
- Ask questions over and over, until you're sure you've heard the answers right. Make sure you aren't overstating the seriousness of even a serious treatment or operation. It may be that this is a way to cure you, not an indication of how life-threatening your illness is.
- Ask nurses and doctors about pain management. Are they prepared to make your life as easy as possible? Ask about visiting hours, about food, about anything that will make you feel better.
- For the family, learn how to soothe yourselves. Take cash (for pay phones, snacks); take a cell phone (some hospitals allow them); take comfort food (a granola bar, plenty of bottled water), because the cafeteria may be closed when you most need it. Take a book for when you want to stay in the room with your wife or mother and she's asleep. And you, too, should not be afraid to ask questions and to make requests, anything to calm yourself and reassure your loved one that all is going to be okay. And don't forget to call people who can take over some of your responsibilities for you!
- Finally, it's important that you not forget the preparations you've made. All these things—the granola bar, the phone change, etc.—should go into a *large manila envelope* with the health proxy, living will, phone

numbers of friends, cash, and anything else you need legally, just in case something happens during an operation or at any other time that causes you to feel they're needed. Mark the envelope "Hospital." [And you just might want to photocopy this chapter and put it there, too. Or even put the whole book into the envelope.]

When Sorrows Come

The time may come when what was chronic becomes acute or, as it must, eventually, for all of us, when we are faced with dying. To a large degree, that crisis is what this book has been about: preparing you for that certainty. If this is a child, you need to look back over the chapter on children. If this is your own crisis, let us repeat what you need to think about:

- Are your decisions about end-of-life care up to date? Have you communicated those thoughts to everyone who needs the information?
- Are your pieces of paper up to date?
- What do you know about palliative care at the hospital where you're headed?
- Have you clearly indicated to your agent at what point you would want to have care withdrawn?
- Have you clearly indicated when you might want to go into hospice care?
- Have you talked with a hospice and made prearrangements for care at home?
- What do you want to do about close friends and family? At what point do you want them to come to see you? What kind of support do you want?
- What are you thinking of doing about emotional and spiritual support?

When Is It Over?

It may come as a surprise to you that we do not always know when someone is dying. Especially when the miracles of modern medicine allow many chances to try something new, or to allow for remissions, or for "one more day," knowing when someone is actually in their last days or hours is not something that every physician can know. In fact, most people, including health professionals, often make mistakes about such prognoses.

If you are going to put into practice some of the things we have spoken about in this book, then you are going to want to know when it is too late for curative care; when hospice is warranted; when to think about removing life support; when to take over the decisionmaking; when to rally the family around; and, especially, when to have good heart-to-heart talks with your loved ones.

But if you and your physician don't know how long someone may live, this may prove difficult.

Psychologically, you will want to have lead time for all these events. But you or your loved one may come in and out of consciousness, or have periods of lucidity, or have months or relative stability or lack of pain. In short, time may be very flexible. This is hard to deal with, and makes decisionmaking very difficult sometimes. However, knowing in advance that this can happen may make it easier for you to prepare for the worst, but live in expectation of a future that may have its ups and downs.

For All Crises

- When you get a bad diagnosis, ask yourself: "Who's in my corner?" "Who should I consult?"
- When there's a recurrence or an emergency, ask yourself if you've called together your team. Don't do any of this thinking alone. Ask your doctor or ask someone else to go over these things with you. There are stages to think about for yourself, and for others. Refer back to other chapters in this book.
- Have you thought about aggressive medications or treatments? Have you thought about inpatient palliative care? Have you thought about hospice?
- No matter when a crisis comes, you should have certain telephone numbers and pieces of paper in your manila envelope: Any 800 numbers that you might need. Friends to help share the caregiving load. Your hospice administrator's number. Your spiritual counselor's number.

14

DNRs and Assisted Dying

There is a ton of misinformation about what happens during the final stages of a person's life. For an agent or family member to rest easy about making decisions, it's important that all misinformation—or as much as possible—be dispelled. We cannot do justice to every fact surrounding the last days or weeks of life, but we can give a few important facts about some myths—myths that stand in the way of a family's comfort, and that of the dying person's.

You might expect that a primary care physician, oncologist, or palliative care specialist would supply information about some of these things, or that the hospital social worker would do so, helping families to understand what lies ahead. Ideally, that *would* happen. But often doctors—as we have suggested previously—have as tough a time facing such truths as we do. And when it's crucial to pick up all the pieces, at the end of the end, there just isn't enough time and energy: There just aren't enough social workers and others who know the score to fill you in.

So read now, and let this material become part of the knowledge base that will help see you through the final days of an illness or disease.

The Truth about CPR and DNRs

Let's start with the truth about CPR—cardiovascular resuscitation. This is a long-worded term for what emergency medical system (EMS) and other emergency workers do when a person has a heart attack or stops breathing. If this happens during our normal lives, say at a meal at a restaurant or in the midst of other daily activities, someone would call 911 and want them to respond immediately with skilled help. You want them to get your heart started at once, to take you to the hospital to check out why you had the trouble you had, to make sure that you can go on with your life.

But what if you have a terminal disease? What if you are at home, being tended by a private nurse and/or hospice workers? Or you are in your hospital bed and your family is waiting for your death, having accepted that there is no point in prolonging life anymore? What's more, what if you have put into your living will and instructed your agent that "I do not want to be resuscitated if there is nothing that can be done to allow me a return to *quality* life?" In other words, what if you have made a decision that you want to die as normally as possible, without a last-minute rescue, if all that rescue would do is leave you in bed to await the next stoppage of breathing or of your heart, and the next, and the next?

You might be interested in what a physician from a hospital in a middle-sized community has to say about DNRs. It was posted in a Last Acts Partnership online discussion group:

My name is Marti Haykin, I am a neurology resident, and I have just joined the Last Acts discussion group. I am a member of the Bioethics Committee at my hospital, and I am spearheading a project to help educate my fellow physicians on "How to discuss 'Do Not Resuscitate'/'Do Not Intubate' orders with patients and their families." There seems to be a lot of misunderstanding, among physicians, nurses, patients, and families, about situations in which resuscitative efforts should NOT be initiated. Part of the confusion comes from television programs which show CPR as a dramatic but usually successful procedure (and most people do not know that the success rate of CPR for both in and out-of-hospital cardiac arrests is about 12%). Unfortunately, a lot of confusion is the result of physicians not recognizing that CPR and other emergency efforts are simply *not* likely to benefit certain patients and will only prolong the dying process.

I personally have witnessed far too many cases in which attempts at "resuscitation" have only led to needless pain and suffering. CPR and other interventions are life-saving in many situations—but physicians need to improve their ability to communicate to patients and families that "resuscitation" is not *always* in the patient's best interest.

Dr. Haykin goes on to say that many hospitalized patients are never informed of the possible risks of such efforts to resuscitate, including broken ribs, bruises to the heart, damage to the liver, brain injury, even a permanent vegetative state. It couldn't be stated more clearly. If you agree, you and your agent need to know three items of procedure:

1. *In the hospital:* Unless otherwise instructed by physicians through a DNR (Do Not Resuscitate) order, personnel at a hospital will attempt to restart your heart or put you on artificial breathing apparatus. A "Code Blue" will be called. Electric shock may be applied to your body to get everything back in running condition. You might be given a variety of tubes to keep things flowing smoothly.

2. *Outside a hospital setting:* Even if you have gotten a physician to sign a DNR for a hospital setting, if you are in trouble and an EMS crew is called, they must use CPR and other life-saving procedures unless you have also procured a special kind of statement: a "non-hospital" (or out-of-hospital) DNR order. These are orders signed by a physician that can be presented to emergency medical personnel, that allow them not to begin resuscitation. Currently forty-four states and the District of Columbia have authorized the use of non-hospital DNR orders.

3. *Both in and out of hospital:* Many health care personnel, because of their training or their own belief systems, may insist on using CPR unless your agent can immediately prove that you did not and do not want it. This may require an agent having a copy of the health care proxy with him or her during these last days, *and* being present when any changes in your condition require it.

The ramifications can be serious. While there is no real difference for most of us between being *withdrawn* from artificial breathing apparatus and not being put *on* the apparatus in the first place, some institutions will make it harder to *remove* artificial breathing or feeding tubes than if they were asked not to start them in the first place. This may be because of a mistaken belief that one or another religion descries a difference between acts of omission and commission. While trying such an intervention may make everyone feel less guilty then and later ("We didn't even *try* to save her"), you and your agent should discuss this issue thoroughly.

We said earlier that many of us will not die in a flash: we won't be "taken" at the first sign of disease. In this world of increasingly greater survival with chronic illnesses, there will be many in-between situations: people may wander in and out between ill and relative good health. Even during the last days, to know when someone is truly dying or when they are only at a relative low point in their illness is often difficult.

Arthur Fletcher, a long-time resident of the South Side of Chicago, was suffering from Hodgkin's disease. He and his family had long ago come to terms with the fact that he would not be able to stay alive much longer, and he and they had agreed that when the time came, he would want to die at home, without extraordinary measures. One day while out walking with a supportive friend, he became short of breath. He sank to the pavement, and his friend knew the end had come—suddenly, unexpectedly. But a neighbor called 911, and Fletcher ended up in the emergency room of a local hospital, on artificial breathing apparatus. His family came to the hospital and had to fight to have the ventilator removed, so Fletcher could die naturally.

In short, the best intentions of a health care worker may keep you and your agent from seeing to it that you receive exactly the care or lack of care that you prefer.

Lukas's Story _____

When I got to the point that I knew I was going into the hospital for the operation, I made it clear to everyone involved exactly what I wanted in terms of end-of-life care, in case something went wrong. On the issue of DNR, for instance, I reminded my wife under what circumstances I would or would not want to be kept alive, and I wrote the following to the surgeon—whom I knew from only one meeting:

Because you and I are new to each other, a word about my end-of-life wishes. If something should happen during the operation that renders me unconscious, my wife, Susan, is my proxy. If something happens that would render me permanently unable to resume a "normal" life, and especially if I were unconscious and not likely to resume consciousness, I do not want to be resuscitated if my heart or other functions should falter. In short, please insert a DNR into my record at that point.

At the hospital, before the operation, the surgeon acknowledged he had received the note, and thanked me for it.

———————————

A note: occasionally a physician wants you to have a DNR when you don't want one. You and your agent have every right *not* to have a DNR, just as you have the right to have one!

The Truth about Artificial Hydration and Nutrition

When Alice R. was ninety-four, her heart began to give out. She went into a nursing home to await her last days. Alice had written a living will and made her daughter her agent, so it was the daughter who made sure that a DNR was in place at the nursing home, and that the staff knew her mother's wishes about extreme measures. One thing that had not been discussed or investigated specifically was the tendency of people whose death is imminent not to be hungry or thirsty. To outsiders, especially family members, the inability or refusal to eat is upsetting. They want staff to "do something" about it.

And, in fact, Alice R. did begin to refuse food. She could still communicate with her family, much of which took the form of complaints about being in a strange setting. Her daughter assumed that her mother was still very much alive and should be force-fed. Otherwise, she felt, it was akin to starving her mother to death.

But the nursing home staff knew otherwise. They knew that when patients eat less and less in the face of a serious illness, it is often because death is in fact near. In this case, forcing food or drink on the patient can actually cause distress; it can interfere with the ability to breathe properly.

Most physicians will tell you that the placement of a tube—except to solve a very temporary problem, such as a swollen throat or other impediment to feeding an otherwise hungry or thirsty patient—is almost always just a delaying tactic; the patient will soon die anyway—in distress, because of the feeding tube.

Armed with the truth about her mother's reticence to eat, Alice's daughter concluded that her mother did not want "artificial hydration or nutrition," in other words, did not want a tube placed in her abdomen or in her nose to give food or liquids, if the only purpose of such a device was to delay her death—a death that was coming on its own soon. She summoned family members to the bedside to say good-bye.

Being informed and aware of the truth about artificial hydration—that at the every end of life, it is not useful, and can even be harmful—helped tremendously. Alice's family was able to stop being afraid that they were starving their loved one, and start thinking about how to say good-bye.

On the other hand, sometimes nursing home personnel are not as well informed or thoughtful as were those who cared for Alice R. Often, apparently with the best of intentions, personnel may express dismay: "Are you going to *starve* your father?" These are gut-wrenching questions, and agents may find themselves under the stress of facing the imminent death of a treasured person while being bombarded with guilt-provoking demands for instant decisionmaking. It's not unusual for an agent to find herself unable to act at these vulnerable moments. The more you arm your agent with knowledge and reassurance that these are *your* decisions that he or she is implementing, the easier the job will be.

One more thing: In July 2003, the *New England Journal of Medicine* reported on a study in Oregon of the small number of people who had *actively* sought to end their lives by refusing to eat or drink. The nurses who tended them said that such deaths were, in their view, "very good deaths," free of distress and suffering. This should be reassuring to those whose loved ones may simply stop eating and drinking as death nears.

As the next section will show, we are neither suggesting nor urging that patients near the end of life commit suicide by refusing to eat or drink. The simple fact is that it is not the worst way to die.

The Truth about Assisted Dying

For some, it's "assisted suicide," for others, "assisted dying," for still others, "euthanasia" or "mercy killing." Whatever you call it, it's become one of the great controversies of our time, one that begins to approach the chaos of discussions about abortion. Those who support some form of assisted dying believe that every person has the right to determine when he or she will die, and that society does not have the right to force people to live with a serious disease that robs them of every normal experience, that puts them into a helpless position, that causes them emotional and psychological pain.

On some level, this book would seem to second that opinion. After all, we have devoted a book to supporting your autonomy during your dying months and days. Why not have autonomy in deciding exactly *when* you will die?

In fact, there are many strong arguments against assisted dying with which we find ourselves in sympathy. The first deals with our right and desire to change our mind once we actually become very, very ill. Here's what one government study found:

> It is difficult for people to fully imagine what a prospective health state might be like. Once they experience that health state, they may find it more or less tolerable than they imagined. Both patients with and patients without a living will were more likely to change their preferences and desire increased treatment once they became hospitalized, suffered an accident, became depressed, or lost functional ability or social activity.
>
> Secondly, there are many ethical arguments against taking your own life, much less giving others the right to do so in concert with you or a surrogate. To take only one example, the Jewish religion has, for millennia, held that our duty is to *preserve* life, not to end it. And while it is true that Judaism supports the elimination of pain and suffering, it does *not* support that elimination by ending your own, or someone else's, life.

The American Medical Association warns that "things can go very wrong once physicians, the guardians of life, become dispensers of death. Our duty to the sick is to heal them or, when this is no longer possible, to care for them; it is not to kill them."

Here are more of our reasons for *not* supporting assisted dying:

- Giving a physician the legal right to help you end your life opens up a whole realm of possibilities of misuse. In countries that have sanctioned euthanasia or assisted dying, accusations of unethical use of such powers have surfaced time and again. The possibility that a family member might wish to hasten another's death for reasons other than empathy always remains open.

- Physical pain and increasing decrepitude are often cited as the chief reasons why assisted dying is necessary: the argument goes that sometimes when we can't cure, the downward trend of the disease leaves people helpless, a burden to others, in pain, or otherwise suffering from intolerable symptoms. As we have suggested elsewhere in this book, medication and other palliative elements can, in most cases, alleviate such symptoms so that the dying person can communicate with loved ones again, and can experience some modicum of quality of life.

- Then there's emotional pain. Many of those seeking the use of a Jack Kevorkian or other person to assist with dying claim that it is the emotional burden of being a "nonperson" more than pain that makes them want to seek a quick way out of life. This is, of course, difficult to comprehend if you haven't been there yourself, which few of us have. Nevertheless, even though life may seem to have no use for a person, psychiatrists often find that what the person is suffering from, in addition to his or her illness, is actually clinical depression. What may be missing is familial support, comfort care, in short, the kind of care that hospice can offer. Antidepressants can be used to make an otherwise suicidal person feel life is worth living a few more years or months.

But what about that small percent who are *not* helped by pain and other symptom relief, for whom antidepressants come too late or too little? What about the cases of ALS, when bodily function is no longer possible, when the mind is alive, but the body is useless? What possible harm could there be in allowing such a person—with or without the aid of a physician—to terminate life?

That question may be more appropriate to a book on religious, moral, and ethical issues than this one, but we're going to take a stab at it.

Suicide itself leaves a trail of sorrow and anger behind it. Even when family and friends know that the person wants to die because living is just too,

too painful, there remains for most of us a disbelief that this beloved person would take him or herself out of our lives. There is something about the suicidal act that leaves those left behind in a state of emotional turmoil, even when they have known of your decision ahead of time.

Second, we feel there is something dangerous in making assisted dying legal; it opens up the possibility of a misuse or corruption of the process, and invites people to choose death as a way out of financial or emotional problems when ill.

We heard the following story from a Chicago man whose uncle was ninety.

I got a call from my uncle George one morning quite early, about five years ago. He wanted me to come see him about something important. George had married late in life (his second marriage) to my Aunt Phyllis. For fifteen years, they lived in a large apartment while my uncle continued his lifelong career, teaching painting. Phyllis had died about five years before this, and George had continued his work until recently. His legs had begun to hurt, and I got the feeling he wasn't doing too well. A year before this date, he had to go into the hospital. He had lost one kidney many years earlier, and his doctor thought something might be going wrong with the remaining one. As it turned out, they discovered not only a spot on his kidney, but a tumor in his brain. The tumor he had actually known about for years, and it had not grown in all that time, but the spot on his kidney was new.

They released George from the hospital, but told him they wanted to keep an eye on that kidney—and on the brain. When I arrived at George's apartment, he was sitting very quietly on a couch. His demeanor told me he was not happy. But I was still not prepared for his request. "You know doctors," he said. "Can you help me get enough sleeping medicine to kill myself?"

For at least an hour, I tried to find out where this sudden depression had come from. More and more, as I listened, I was convinced that the pain in his legs and his general unhappiness were due in part to the death of Phyllis, and to the fact that he really felt his career was over and that he was alone and useless. I argued with him—to no avail. He made me promise I'd accompany him to his physician to help "get the pills."

As soon as I left the apartment, I phoned Uncle George's son, who lived in Philadelphia, and asked him to fly in to join me at the doctor's the next day. Together, we listened to George tell the doctor how sick he was, how he knew he was dying, and how he didn't want to live with that knowledge; he didn't want to be helpless, alone, and in pain. Then he said how he would appreciate it if the doctor would give him the pills he needed. The doctor was so astonished that he stood up and paced the room; he didn't sit down for the rest of the session. "I can't do that," he said, and added that as far as he knew George wasn't that sick. The kidney was stable, so was the brain tumor, and his legs were fine. George was adamant, and he turned to me and said, "*You'll* help me kill myself, won't you?" I said no, I wouldn't. Angrily, he looked me in the eye and asked, "Don't you love me enough to do that?" I responded, "I love you too much to do it."

Suddenly Uncle George looked puzzled. Apparently he didn't know which way to go. I asked the doctor to prescribe some antidepressant medication for my uncle. (I couldn't understand why the doctor hadn't thought of that on his own.) Prozac was prescribed, and I took my uncle home to his apartment. I was worried about him, but his son promised to look after him.

The next day, I phoned from a business trip and was startled to hear my uncle's voice in an entirely different tone. He was "over" the problem, he said. I knew that the Prozac could not have acted that fast. What was going on here? A psychiatrist friend of mine said that maybe my uncle had decided to kill himself anyway; often, an elated tone like that can mean that a depressed person has made a serious decision and now has a plan and can go ahead with that plan. But George insisted that he had been inspired by what the doctor had said—that he wasn't sick—and that "everything was fine."

Was that true? Had there been a miraculous turnaround from the depressed man who wanted to kill himself to the ninety-year-old bon vivant I was hearing?

That was four years ago. In the interim, George has had a hip replacement, has gone to Europe four times to teach seminars, has moved to a little town downstate. He is still going strong, still very happy, still—alive. I have come to the conclusion that Uncle George simply felt abandoned, alone. When I said that I loved him too much to help him die, and his son came in from Philadelphia, and his doctor, too, renewed interest in him, George's desire to die was transformed. What a terrible shame it would have been if the doctor had looked at George—and agreed with him that it was better to die.

The bottom line is, when given the proper attention and treatment, whether it be love or Prozac or morphine, a wish for an assisted death can turn into a wish to go on with life.

Oregon is the only state in the United States that has legally authorized assisted dying. Since the law came into being in the late 1990s, over ninety terminally ill persons have ended their lives that way. There are still arguments in Oregon on both sides of the issue, and a recent federal attack on the law has thrown it into the courts yet once again.

It may be worth keeping an eye on Oregon to see how it fares in this regard. Is the right to death absolute on the part of terminally ill people? Or are palliative care, human relationships, and familial love valuable weapons in the arsenal against the depression and loneliness brought down upon a small but important minority of those who die with long-term, debilitating illnesses?

15

FINANCES

Throughout this book we have tried to stay away from financing and funding difficulties because we wished to look at best health care practices. But it would be irresponsible of us not to acknowledge, even in abbreviated fashion, that money is as much—or more of—a problem in medical care, and especially end-of-life care, as it is in the rest of our lives.

Any cursory reading of the newspapers will tell you that the costs of medical care in the United States are going up, and no one seems to know what to do about that. Stories abound on the high price of medicines, of technological innovations, of physicians. At the same time, we learn that Medicare is in trouble, and that the government must, in order to meets its budgetary requirements, diminish reimbursements to hospitals and doctors. This, in turn, has led to occasional revolts on the part of physicians or physicians' groups against working for reduced fees. And, as many find out firsthand, the state-federal partnership in medical support for lower-income people (Medicaid) often cannot be accessed because many doctors and hospitals or clinics will not accept Medicaid patients.

Inside the world of end-of-life care, these troubles are multiplied. Where training does not exist, it is hard to find funding to begin it; where certain kinds of care are not available, it's hard to persuade the government(s) to fund them.

The Institute of Medicine paper on children's palliative care referred to in chapter 11 states, "Children's palliative care requires appropriate financing, including the development of new methods of reimbursement within the context of a changing health care financing system."

That's a special problem because private and public insurances often oversimplify the situation and say that when you go into hospice you should no longer get curative care. Providing end-of-life care that involves a mix of palliative, curative, and preventive care could be very expensive. Hospice programs frequently find themselves without the resources to take care of these children without going into the red. In addition, since most of the patients in hospice are adults, many programs are not geared to handle an infant or a toddler or a teenager, all of whom bring very different kinds of needs than people in their seventies and eighties.

That doesn't mean finding coverage as an adult is easy. Without long-term health insurance or someone to look after you at home, many adults with chronic or terminal illnesses go without the kind of care they need, whether it be normal, experimental, palliative, or supportive.

How can we change all that?

We believe that with appropriate care, with appropriate interest, and with appropriate innovation, it is sometimes possible to make financing appear where it didn't seem to exist before. Here's what Dr. Ross Hayes of the Children's Hospital and Regional Medical Center in Seattle had to say:

> I think I've been invited here from Seattle to talk a little bit about one of those small steps around the country that's working . . . Palliative Care Service at Children's Hospital in Seattle. Palliative care is simply good care. It's giving children what they need, when they need it. Sometimes it's a combination of curative measures, supportive measures, but until now the current system hasn't been very good at providing that type of care and it has been even harder to get that type of care financed. In Seattle, we've begun to find a way by partnering with our insurance plan partners.
>
> Let me tell you a little bit about how this has worked. We have worked together with Blue Cross and Blue Shield and the Washington State Department of Social and Health Services Medical Assistance Program to address children's needs, children who have potentially life-limiting illnesses, and with the help of a grant from The Robert

Wood Johnson Foundation, we were able to develop an innovative approach. What we did was this. We went to these two large private insurers and our state-funded health care agency and we asked them to open up their benefits plan and to think of it in a new way, and the way that it worked was based on the idea of case management and care coordination. Starting in the mid 1990s, we went to our families of dying children and we asked them, "What is it that you really need?" and over and over we got the same answer back. Families said we need care coordination. One mother said I have health care professionals crawling all over my child. It's an army and I need a general to direct all of this care. And one way or another we heard that over and over again. Unfortunately case management, community case management, is very rarely reimbursed, so in this innovative approach, what we did was assigned a case manager in the community to the family and child and also identified a similar case manager at the insurance plan. We had the two of them work together in what we called co-case management.

The second innovation was what we call flexible administration of the benefits plan. It works like this: I think of a benefits package being something like a house. It's what your employer bought for you from the insurance plan. It may include this. It may not include that. It's a house that has all kinds of walls in it, some of which are artificial barriers that make the delivery of care harder. For example, if you go into the hospice room, you have to promise to die in six months. If you don't, you get shoved into another room. If you want hospice, you have to give up dialysis. If you want a special technical process from the home health care agency, you may not be able to get that from a hospice nurse. So there are all these artificial walls in the house. The insurance plans bravely said we'll keep the house the same size, but we'll tear down the walls, and if you tell us what to do, we'll do our very best to try to deliver the services you need regardless of what your benefit package walls and regulations say. So we studied that. We did that for four years and we studied thirty families for three years and this is what we found. It was a win-win-win situation. The families felt that they had better care. Children had less visits to the emergency department, less intensive care unit stays, families were more satisfied with the care that they received, and they were more satisfied with their relationship with their health plan. We as providers were happier because we didn't have to fight with the insurance companies all the time. It saved a lot of time and effort and the insurance plans were more satisfied because believe it or not, there are human beings who work in insurance companies. Many of them are nurses and they enjoy the fact that they are able to deliver added value, more quality care, and guess what? It didn't cost any more.

What we found by doing this flexible administration of benefits was that by tailoring the needs to the individual child, tailoring the care to the child's individual needs, we were actually able to (in most cases) spend the same amount that we would have otherwise, or often spend less, and many, many times, much, much less. So this was a nice way to approach this problem, and you know what, it did not take rocket science. It did not take a lawsuit and it did not take any appropriation of new money. This is what it took. It took the willingness on our part and on the plan's part to think outside the box and to be creative, to be innovative. It took a certain amount of courage on the part of the health plans to try something new. We sat in meetings with these people every Thursday morning for six months, trying to explain what we needed, and everybody thought it was a good idea and when we got around to actually signing a memorandum of understanding, the plan said, "Oh, well, we can't actually do that" and we said, "Why not?" and they said, "Well, we've never done that before." And so it took courage for them to step out and to take a risk and most of all, what it took was trust, that rare and becoming rarer and rarer commodity in health care where the insurance companies trusted that community case manager to represent the needs of that child adequately and ask for what that child needed, not the moon, but what that child needed. And it took trust on the part of the families and the case managers and us to believe that the plans would do the very best that they could to deliver the care that that child needed.

We went on at such length about this work because it is the kind of innovative, flexible thinking that may be required to make changes in our health care system on all fronts, but especially in end-of-life care. It may be that as this book is published, children's hospice care will no longer require any mention of the six months' rule. This would be enormous progress.

Such progress is possible in other arenas, permitting certain curative interventions while keeping up palliative work, for instance. Often it requires the work of special experts and groups to raise our consciousness about these matters. But it also requires that we, the health care consumers, embrace the cause, educate ourselves about the issues, and demand more from government and the private sector.

16

GIVE GRIEF A CHANCE

The writers of Ecclesiastes were right: there is a time to mourn, and it's an important time. Grieving is healthy—as long as it doesn't go on too long. But Americans have a peculiar slant on grief. We can be very open about it at funerals—though not as open as some other cultures; we can also be very formal about it, or spend a lot of money on shows of grief. But most Americans believe that—for good taste, good health, and good self-discipline—it should be short-lived. We seem to feel embarrassed or unable to cope when mourning goes on beyond a proscribed period.

In fact, many believe that grieving goes on "too long" if it lasts more than a couple of months. Experts, on the other hand, believe that's way too short! Though we acknowledge that different people grieve in different ways and for different reasons, psychologists and other experts are clear about one thing: *a year* is none too long a period for some form of mourning and grieving to go on after the death of a loved one. This has a good basis in psychology and in religion. A year passes; the anniversary comes around; a sense of a closed cycle settles in. No wonder that religions like Judaism actually prescribe a yearlong period of mourning. And if the death is particularly gruesome, or that of a young child, or any other number of cases, grief can go on beyond that.

How Long is Too Long?

Everyone heals at his or her own pace. However, if one of the two following things happens, then perhaps mourning has persisted longer than it should or it has taken hold on you or someone you know beyond its "normal" state. Then you may be in the grip of depression or something psychologists call "complicated bereavement."

- If your mourning persists beyond a year, pretty much unabated.
- If, over the course of the first year, your pain does not at least begin to diminish; if you cannot stop crying and thinking about the loved one; and if you cannot carry on normal work and normal relationships.

If this happens, it is worth thinking about seeking professional help.

Beyond this kind of guideline, however, there is nothing wrong with crying occasionally over the death of a loved one—even though it may have happened two, three, six months previously, or even more than a year ago. Everyone heals at a different pace.

Why Is Grief Important?

The finality of death creates a kind of loss that is unlike any other. This loss can be the most profound experience of life and also the most painful. Bereavement, as the expression of that pain, is part of a healing or reconciliation process enabling us to continue to function in the world.

To a large extent, we have already begun to discuss this important process in chapter 9, where we talked about emotional and spiritual reconciliation. Families and other loved ones are already beginning to grieve during the time when a patient is dying. How you deal with the dying process—whether you absent yourself out of fear and denial, or participate in some deeply emotional way—may have an important influence on how long and how well you will deal with sorrow *after* death. There is ample evidence that those who have had time to say good-bye, do better than those who did not. Suicides and traumatic accidental deaths leave those left behind with more troublesome grieving periods than those in which long illnesses have given families time for reconciliation and saying farewell.

Similarly, people who have complicated relationships—love and antagonism alternating—often find that the grieving process is deeper and more painful, not to mention longer, than people whose relationships have been more straightforward. Even a good old-fashioned anger that is unmixed with love leaves a friend or relative with less complicated emotions at the time of death than a love–hate relationship.

We have also dealt with the important issue of children and the mourning process in chapter 11, where we discussed how crucial it is to attend to their needs. How wise they can be! We may have a few decades on them, but that doesn't mean we understand how to grieve any better than they do. The parent whose spouse has died may think he or she needs to be strong for the sake of the child. The fact is that "strength" or stoicism may turn out to be a real impediment to getting through the grieving process. Letting children in on the process, letting go of your own control, crying, experiencing your grief, and not being too hard on yourself ("It's time to get back to work. I've spent too much time on grief already!") are all key elements in achieving a better outcome to the death of a loved one.

For the truth is that even if you have been at the bedside, said good-bye a dozen times, or given of yourself during six months or six days of painful dying of a loved one, you need time to grieve, to adjust, to come to terms with the absence of someone you cared about.

And wouldn't it be wonderful if we all recognized how serious grieving is; if people let us mourn and didn't expect us to be back at work in two days, all smiles? One sixteen-year-old, whose school friends just didn't get it, explains her distress over feeling alone in her grief:

> It's difficult to introduce the subject of death. People don't come around saying, "How are you feeling today? Are you feeling weepy or whatever?" No. People that I thought were my best friends in the whole world would just say "Oh, hi, how ya doing? Bye." Those were the people I always depended on, and they were gone.

The Signs of Grief

- *Crying.* We are all aware of the sadness that accompanies the loss of something or someone important to us. Heaviness in our body, tears, the inability to take joy in what's going on in the rest of our lives: these are familiar signs and feelings of grief. But some of the other emotions and behavior are not necessarily as recognizable. And some are downright frightening.

- *Anger.* Anger comes as a surprise to many, yet it's a very common reaction to loss, and a part of many people's grief. When someone we love dies, we often feel as if we have been attacked at our core. Many times the death comes as a surprise—a nasty surprise—and we may react to it as we react to nasty surprises in the past—with anger. Sometimes we blame others for the death, and that makes us full of rage, too. Sometimes it's just a matter of being too tired and too sad to cope with one more request, whether from a family member or the funeral home, or God knows whom.

- *Guilt.* Some deaths catch us so much by surprise that we feel we should or could have done something to prevent them. Did an accident occur because we weren't there to stop it? Were the doctors the right doctors, and should we have been more aggressive in finding others? These feelings can lead to a strange sense of guilt in those left behind, a guilt that is hard to talk about and hard to dispense with. To tell you that your guilt is natural may be of no help, but we can tell you it certainly isn't useful to you, and probably totally unjustified. If it doesn't go away, get some counseling help.

- *Hopelessness.* Sadness can turn into depression. Hopelessness, which is a common initial reaction after the death of someone who was a main support to you, can become unnatural and harmful if it goes on too long.

- *"I'm going crazy."* It's not uncommon for those left behind to "see" the dead person on the street in front of them; to dream about strange things; to feel spaced out, undefined, unuseful, incompetent. None of these are signs of going crazy. None of these—and other feelings besides—are surprising. Death is a shock, and our reaction to it can be outsized and bizarre. As long as these feelings eventually subside, you are probably in the normal range of grief.

- *Numbness.* Sometimes, despite the importance of the person who died, we don't actually fall into a great sadness or despair or fit of crying. Instead, we are *un*feeling. This numbness can come as a disturbing shock to us. We may feel that we *should* be in tears or tearing our hair out. We *should* behave or feel as others do, with their clear-cut signs of grief. But there are no *shoulds* when it comes to grief. Any and all reactions are common to some and uncommon to others. All are natural.

- *The anniversary blues.* Even though grief usually abates after a year or so, many people find themselves reexperiencing some of the same emotions at the same pitch as earlier on. This can be surprising and dismaying. "I thought I was over this!" is not an unknown reaction. However, for some people, anniversaries are times when they do react more adversely and with memories of sorrow. This, too, is natural.
- *Men versus women.* One of the stranger facts about grief is how differently men and women often feel and react. It is not uncommon to hear a wife complain that her husband doesn't feel sad because he doesn't show it. Or for a husband to complain that his wife is always in tears. These gender differences are very well known, and while expressions of grief aren't the same for all men and all women, it would not be surprising to find men behaving "stoically" while women are more open about their grief.

The Patient Grieves, Too

Many people may be surprised to find grief: in the patient.

Dr. Linda Emanuel says this:

Patients themselves have to go through a kind of grief process every time they lose a function, and every time they lose the hope of a certain piece of their future: They lose the hope of being there five years from now. They lose the hope of being able to write with their own hand as opposed to dictating the letter that they wanted to leave behind for their daughter to open after they were gone. Whatever it is that they have to let go of, they're going through a grief process from the moment that they have a diagnosis. That's the first big grief step: they have to let go of the idea of immortality. From there on grief is happening to the person who is challenged by an illness. If we professionals don't understand that, we're going to be missing a big piece of caring for someone.

This idea that not only we, the family and friends, mourn the loss of the patient, but that the patient him/herself does so helps explain why it is often difficult to console a terribly sick or dying person. We may not realize that what is going on is not just fear (terrible as that may be), not just anger, not just doubt and dismay, but inconsolable grief.

How can we deal with the patient's grief? In many ways, the answer is exactly how we should deal with our *own* grief: allow the patient to talk about his or her loss and not to console or contradict ("You're fine, I know you are") or do anything that gets in the way of that grief. Here is how one patient expressed it:

> I have been having feelings of depression, but I think I'm better. And I think talking about it has helped. Just to say it out loud. And to hear that it's okay to feel depressed—that it's understandable. That's helpful.

And Doctors, Too

One more surprise—at least to many people—is that doctors who care for dying people also grieve the loss of their patients. This is not just a professional cry of "Oh, I failed." It can and often is genuine grief. After all, many patients form a close relationship with their physician(s) over a long period of time. And despite the complaints that often emanate from us—that our doctors "don't care" about us, or that managed care has taken the humanity out of our medical care—physicians are human. Here's how one oncologist, Dr. Jamie von Roenn, talks about handling her grief. She is a professor of medicine in Chicago, and also works with many individual patients:

> I allow myself to feel sad, actually. I think if you don't, then you never recover from all the losses. And for people I care about a lot, I do what I do for a friend who dies. I go to the funeral and I call the family and I do the things that you do with people that you care about. I don't go to every funeral, but if I feel the need to, then I go. I've learned not to go to please other people. I write everybody letters, but I don't go to them all.
>
> I think the only way to walk away from someone dying and not feel horrible is to feel like I did everything I could as a doctor and everything I could as a human being and that's all there is. I can't do anything else. And so there's some sense of, well, I tried. But I think if you don't give as a human being there's a certain emptiness about that, and I think that's how people get burned out. I don't think there's such a thing as giving too much. I don't think you ever get hurt like that, as long as you have a balance in your life.

The Rest of Us

And so, having recognized that it's important to allow the patient to grieve and to allow physicians to grieve, what about the rest of us? How do we deal with loss in such a way that we can move on with our lives, but without giving up what we feel is due the person to whom we were close?

First, as we suggested above, is to allow ourselves time, and to allow others time. Many people are familiar with the tales about one of a pair of twins who dies and how the remaining twin is left feeling as if he has been robbed of a part of his very self. The closeness of twins is so evident that we understand the grief that might follow such a death. And we may not suggest they hasten their period of mourning to make our lives less bothersome.

But we don't always understand a similar tearing apart that occurs when a mother or grandmother dies, especially if the person left behind is an adult. Despite the lip service given to funerals and other forms of grieving, even spouses are expected to "get over" the death of a wife or husband after a few months, even if they've been married for a long time. Often we hear a friend suggesting, "It's time. Why don't you go out and date?" We may even worry that our loved ones are "sinking" into a depression if they stare off into the distance or refuse an invitation to go out for the evening. The phrase, "Go ahead, kids, I'm okay by myself" is considered a symptom rather than a statement that reflects the need for a little more time by a grieving spouse to be alone, to continue the mourning process.

Second, face the fact that many people are uncomfortable around grief if they don't themselves feel the pain deeply. This discomfort may, actually, be the biggest detriment to giving people the chance to mourn properly. We want our friends and family to come back from their sadness, to be "themselves" again. It will make *us* feel more comfortable.

Third, accept the fact that you have to "work through" grief. It is psychologically healthy—almost imperative—to work through grief, not to bury it. Take the case of Marcia Lattanzi-Licht, whose daughter Ellen died in a car accident with a drunken driver. The girl was seventeen. At first, Ms. Lattanzi-Licht was distraught. It was, without doubt, the worst thing that had ever happened to her. And while we have been dealing in this book not with sudden deaths, but with more chronic, long-term illnesses, where one can prepare for the death that follows, Ms. Lattanzi-Licht's tale has many, many lessons for us.

There was a time when my grief was so loud I could barely stand the noise. I remember the physical blow of hearing she was dead. I couldn't catch my breath and I couldn't stop crying. It seemed as if someone had set off a bomb that destroyed the house of my life.

Everywhere I looked, there was loss. Its hallmarks are a sense of shock and numbness, a feeling of being alone, and a desolation that I never thought I'd have to feel. My thinking was scattered, and I felt like an animal prowling, trying to protect what was left of my world. I realized how limited and powerless I was. I felt a crushing burden of sorrow weighing on me.

That is a very good description of grief: everywhere we look, there is loss. This rings true to us, and we must believe that it rings true to anyone reading this book who has lost a loved one, even if it wasn't what must be the most awful loss in the world: a child.

So, now what? How did Marcia Lattanzi-Licht pick up the pieces and move on with her life? For one thing, she recognized that Ellen's younger brother needed her. She also allowed herself to express her anger at the way that Ellen died, anger for her own loss and anger for her son's loss of a sister. Expressing that anger was another way of letting her sorrow have full sway for a while.

At the same time, she felt socially pressured to hold back her tears. It was clear to her that the more often she contained her tears, the more others perceived her as "doing well." Fortunately, many interpreted her tears as a sign of healthy grief, and Lattanzi-Licht states emphatically that across time, the one most important thing that helped her "was the unwavering caring and support that surrounded me."

The Comfort Zone

How can you feel more comfortable with your grief? Who can help? *How* can they help? Each person will find his or her own avenue toward succor during grief. But what follows are some ways in which others have been able to work through the period of mourning.

Hope. Some experts suggest that you look to past losses to remind yourself that what may seem like a hopeless situation now will melt slowly into a more promising one.

Friendship. For millions and millions of people, the relationships they have with friends can prove the ultimate comfort during times of grief.

Family. Even families with strained relationships often find that coming together during times of loss can be helpful.

Withdrawal. Don't be afraid to be alone. It's not a sign of your inability to cope. All of us occasionally need to be by ourselves to nurse our wounds.

Work. Don't be afraid to work. If it gives you comfort, then do it. Don't be afraid that it shows disrespect for the one who died.

Crying. And don't, for God's sake, be afraid to cry. For men, especially, it can be a great relief.

Self-help groups. Occasionally, the form of death can be such that you may need to find others whose loved one has died in a sudden accident, or at an early age, or by suicide. In most cities there are self-help clearing houses that can find for you the right group.

Therapy. For some, the grief doesn't go away, or it doesn't abate when you need it to. Finding the right social worker or pastoral counselor or other therapist is absolutely a good thing to do under these circumstances.

Rituals. As we've suggested elsewhere, the rituals of memorial services, funerals, church and synagogue support—all can be helpful tools for tapping into community and spiritual support.

Taking care of yourself. Movies, theater, sex, massage, sleep, food—all are well-known and legitimate avenues of relief and escape from your grief. The days are long gone when Queen Victoria had to wear black for years in order to prove her grief. And then there's . . .

Humor. It's okay to laugh. It may be the best way for you to find release. It's not disrespectful, though it may be offensive to other friends or family members, so make sure you respect others when they can't laugh with you.

For Lattanzi-Licht, the most important of these were connections to others who allowed her to grieve *and* acknowledged they understood the horror of what had happened to her. "The greatest learning I've had as I've lived with Ellen's death is that no one makes it through a painful time alone."

This is echoed by Dr. Emanuel, whose experience with death and dying is not only professional, but profoundly personal.

We're beginning to realize again that there is no such thing as illness experienced in isolation. It's experienced in association with family members and friends and loved ones and community members. They are a hugely important part of the entire illness experience. They can make it better, they can make it worse, and they themselves can suffer.

As time went by, Lattanzi-Licht was aware of how many people were acknowledging her loss in a number of ways, by coming to the funeral, visiting, sending notes and flowers, bringing food, making phone calls.

There it is. Out of the horror of a drunken accident, the loss of a child, a mother comes through her grief with the support of others. At the same time, she never forgets her daughter. "There continues to be an empty space in my life without her. And yet, all the other parts of my life remain sweet, and perhaps more so with time. Ellen's death has shown me the great depth of caring and compassion that exists in others. The support and love of friends and family continues to be one of the richest parts of my life."

What this story tells us is that a woman who had suffered the worst kind of loss—the loss of a child—needed time to fit that loss into her life. If she had not had the time to grieve properly, if she had not rejected the notion of a quick "recovery," then she might have suffered forever. The second thing that she makes clear is that given that space of time and given caring friends and neighbors, she was able to assimilate the loss of her daughter into her life. She did not forget Ellen. But she did go on with her life, as all of us must do.

Complicated Bereavement

If normal grieving is not permitted or goes awry, medical evidence points to long-term problems. For older adults, the consequences are often physical. They get sick. They die an earlier death. With younger adults, the evidence shows that they have a whole host of psychological problems: depression, anxiety, difficulty in intimate relationships. This analysis comes from a study performed by Grace Christ, Ph.D., at the Columbia University School of Social Work, and is backed up by lots of anecdotal evidence.

So what do you do if mourning goes on too long? While grief is essentially a private experience, as Ms. Lattanzi-Licht has shown, people need some kind of support during mourning, and often that support needs to be beyond that available from family and friends.

- Psychotherapy, counseling, bereavement support groups, or other professional help can provide that support.
- There are good books available on the grief process. Some can be found in the Bibliography at the end of this book.
- The Resources section includes a list of organizations whose purpose is to ease the transition back to "normal" after the death of a loved one.
- Finally, almost every community in America has a variety of forms of counselors, from social workers to clergy to psychiatrists. No one should be ashamed to avail themselves of such counseling.

Post-Traumatic Stress Disorder

Occasionally the trauma that happens to people through the death of a loved one is so dramatic, so outsized, so beyond the normal death, that the survivor experiences what is called post-traumatic stress disorder (PTSD). For a long time, it was thought that only victims of war, rape, devastation by natural forces (such as hurricane or tornado) experienced PTSD. Not so—we all could be victims of this stress-related disorder if the event is particularly traumatic. It is not surprising that after the September 11, 2001, attack on the World Trade Center, thousands of New Yorkers experienced physical ailments as well as psychiatric problems. But recently experts have recognized that several other kinds of experiences can lead to the condition as well, among them:

- A person discovering the body of a parent who has killed himself.
- Being involved in an accident where you survive, but others do not.
- Having young children abducted or murdered.
- Sudden deaths.
- And, most germane for the readers of this book, any time that a death occurs when it was totally unexpected, or it became much more gruesome and disturbing than was expected. This can happen both to children and to adults.

The American Psychological Association has the following to say about PTSD: Individuals who feel they are unable to regain control of their lives, or who experience the following symptoms *for more than a month,* should consider seeking outside professional mental health assistance:

- Recurring thoughts or nightmares about the event.
- Experiencing anxiety and fear, especially when exposed to events or situations reminiscent of the trauma.
- Being on edge, being easily startled or becoming overly alert.
- Feeling depressed, sad and having low energy.
- Experiencing memory problems including difficulty in remembering aspects of the trauma.
- Feeling "scattered" and unable to focus on work or daily activities.
- Having difficulty making decisions.
- Feeling emotionally "numb," withdrawn, disconnected or different from others.
- Not being able to face certain aspects of the trauma, and avoiding activities, places, or even people that remind you of the event.

As you recall, back in chapter 5 we pointed out that hospice considers the family as the unit of care. This means that both during and after an illness, family members are monitored for stress and grief, and hospice provides a year of grief counseling to the family of a patient. If hospice feels that's necessary, then certainly family members and friends should feel it, too. Not just a few days and then "back to work." Not just a few months and then, "I shouldn't be feeling this way now."

Also keep in mind, as a conference on palliative care pointed out a few years ago:

> Bereavement services are the most neglected, particularly as they relate to neonates and miscarriages, which involve very special bereavement issues. It's quite clear . . . that infant deaths and miscarriages have a lifetime impact on women and families. It isn't a matter of "getting over" something. The degree to which that impact is positive or at least not disruptive of family members' lives is very directly related to how much help they get with the bereavement processes. That also applies to siblings as well as to parents and other members of the families. Paying attention can make a difference between a subsequent healthy adjustment to the tragedy versus a response that includes subsequent depression and other problems that disrupt their ability to be productive, happy citizens.

Give yourself and those around you a chance to mourn, and the life you lead from then on is likely to be a much more enjoyable one.

17

Living with Dying

Here are the facts:

Half of the people who are diagnosed with cancer don't die from it.

Millions of people with heart problems, Alzheimer's Disease, AIDS, emphysema, diabetes, and dozens of other ailments do not die when they think they are going to die. They live many months or years beyond their fears—and often beyond their diagnoses.

Remarkably, and Lukas can attest to it, the human psyche is such that in between checkups and new bouts of your illness, it is not difficult to forget that you're a cancer victim, in the same way that diabetes or arthritis sufferers do not suffer all the time. We can't gloss over the fact that many people with chronic illnesses do experience a loss in quality of life. But millions do not.

So what would you do with that time? Quit your job and do all the things you've always wanted to: travel, bungee-jump, write a book? Spend more time with your children or spouse or grandchildren? Get depressed and take to your bed?

Or decide that no matter how much or how little time is given to you, you want to go on as you were: keep working, keep up as if nothing had changed?

Quite often, the decision is entirely up to you.

In this chapter we want to talk about how you make that decision, and look briefly at the ways in which many, many people go on with their lives despite serious disease or illness or accident.

Living the Life You've Always Led

Scarcely a day goes by, as we write this book, that we aren't drawn to one newspaper article or another that deals with this subject matter.

It's April 13, 2002. In the *New York Times* Sunday magazine there is an article about the author Carol Shields (*The Stone Diaries* won her the Pulitzer Prize). In 1998 she was diagnosed with serious breast cancer and, after a mastectomy and chemotherapy, she was still given very little time to live. Then experimental therapy held off the cancer for a while longer. And the writer realized that perhaps she *could* fit another book—another novel—into her life.

She puzzled for a while over her options, but decided that "she didn't want to make radical changes or try to make up for everything she might have missed out on." And then, knowing that she was dying, Carol Shields wrote that other novel. She had a year in which to do it, and at the end of that time, she was still alive.

No precipitous flights to the Congo to see Africa firsthand, no imbibing of enormous amounts of wine; instead, a flight of a different kind—into another novel, the kind of work she had spent a lifetime doing. She simply decided to keep on doing what she had always done, what her life had always been about. She wanted "the usual rhythms of life."

But how do you do that when you know you're dying? How do you manage to participate, not to give in (as you surely have a right to do) to sorrow and self-pity? Let's not downplay how seriously Carol Shields felt about her cancer. For a long time, she *did* cry, she *did* feel as if she couldn't take another step. But, like many in her situation, she found herself supported by a loving husband, a loving family, friends, fans. And she took control of her life again.

So how to keep hope alive? How to keep going?

Let's back up a minute. There are two kinds of situations in which "keeping going" is germane. The first is the kind that hundreds of thousands of us face every year: the discovery of a lethal cancer or heart disease or HIV infection, or any of a dozen other destructive elements in our bodies. For such people, this is a turning point, and they must decide how to deal with their futures.

The second is when a person is diagnosed with a serious, apparently life-threatening disease or ailment and finds that modern medicine can give a respite (through surgery, medications, whatever) or a remission for much longer than expected. Some people with AIDS, heart disease, and some cancers fall into this category.

In a sense, both have to decide how to keep on going, the first for an unspecified but limited amount of time, the second for an unspecified but (perhaps) unlimited amount of time—a second life, as it were.

For those of you who will eventually be diagnosed with a life-threatening disease, the decision as to how to spend your remaining days, weeks, months, or even years is a very personal one.

Kit Meshenberg had metastasized breast cancer and felt strongly about not being seen as "a patient." Others, struck dumb by the unfairness or suddenness of the event that had taken them from the living into the dying, slip into silence or a sullen defiance. Their energy is taken away by the surprise and the trauma; days are spent in searching for solutions that do not necessarily come.

Here is how Kit Meshenberg thought about it: she believed that it was possible to go on with her work and with her social life, and with her "personhood," as she put it.

> The thing is, with the exception of this "little problem" of having cancer, I am a healthy woman. I'm physically fit and mentally fit and I have to trust that I'm going to land on the right side of the statistics. It's not about denial. I don't minimize the seriousness of this and I'm aware of what's going on, but I'm determined to do two things at once—to act realistically *and* optimistically at the same time. One isn't separated from the other. I'm going to do everything possible to fight this disease but, at the same time, I'm not going to let it take over my life. I have a family that I love and I have work that means a lot to me. I'm going to continue to live my life, full tilt, as long as I possibly can.

Dr. Linda Emanuel was not only Kit Meshenberg's employer at EPEC, but a friend. Here's how she interprets Kit's decisionmaking:

> I think that Kit was actually trying to prove a point for other people

and for the hospice and palliative care movement generally as well: living fully and winning. She was always intent on beating this disease, but she was a very giving person and part of making life meaningful for herself was caring for and contributing to other people. In fact, almost the core of what made life meaningful for her perhaps was that. So contributing to other people, the possibility that they could live life fully and perhaps even more fully once they know that death is not so far away, was a gift that she wanted to give. And she wanted to give it to a lot of people.

The person who faces the challenge of keeping on going, the person with a "second life," is more and more common these days, as screening, preventive medicine, and self-examination become more prevalent, not only in the familiar realms of prostate and breast cancers, but in the more mundane worlds of sunscreen and bicycle helmets. Accidents still occur, limbs are lost, skin cancers are discovered, but surgery puts them into remission. The same is true of prostate and breast cancers—sometimes for ten, fifteen years, sometimes for a long time. When Lukas was diagnosed with lymphoma, his oncologist told him, "You'll probably die of something else, not your lymphoma." Years later, when he discovered he had prostate cancer, he was told the same thing. And, again, several years later, when the lymphoma returned, he was told, "We'll wait . . . and watch." More time to live.

Which doesn't mean that Lukas and all the rest of the people who are diagnosed with a potentially life-limiting or threatening disease aren't scared out of their wits. Or don't face an equally daunting psychological and physical challenge.

Here's how one eighty-three-year old man handled this.

Leonard was diagnosed with severely clogged arteries when he was in his seventies, and had become so exhausted and out of breath that he could no longer climb the stairs in his house. The surgeons performed a three-way bypass and sent Leonard home to a six-month stint of recuperation, including physical therapy. Unfortunately for him, Leonard was unwilling to do the daily exercises his therapist prescribed, or to cut back on the cream and butter he dumped into his gourmet cooking.

Born in the Bronx, Leonard was a self-made man. He served in Europe in World War II, married an American Red Cross Lieutenant he met in

Germany, and together they settled into New York life, where Leonard, who had no college education, moved up from mailroom clerk at a book publishing company to president. After turning in a number of successes in publishing over a three and a half decade career, he retired and worked in philanthropic organizations. He and his wife became experts in orchids and bromeliads, traveling to the rain forests to collect specimens, then forming committees to help steer the world toward action against depredation of those same forests.

All this good work stopped when, a few years later, Leonard was hit with a urinary tract infection. In the course of treatment, the doctors discovered that he had advanced prostate cancer. They prescribed hormones and radiation. While Leonard felt that a sentence of death was hanging over him, he had never been one to shun hard work or to leave a job unfinished, and he felt that his life with his wife of over fifty years was not something he wanted to give up. He entered treatment. In the next few years, into his ninth decade, he was again able to do volunteer work, this time throwing himself into plans to bring the local hospital up to snuff. He "went to the office" three days a week.

Then, while going to his volunteer job, he suddenly felt short of breath and fell down, vomiting. At the hospital, the diagnosis was, yet again, clogged arteries. He would have to an immediate operation, including replacing two veins in his neck.

It was at this point that Leonard asked himself whether this repeated attempt to stay alive was worth it. Why should he put himself and his wife through endless operations, endless medication, endless doctors, countless tests, exhausted days and nights? Why not use the suggestions of the Hemlock Society and end it all?

"What happened at that moment, when I was between throwing in the towel and going for yet another operation, was that I realized that Jane doesn't know how to balance the checkbook. How could I possibly die and leave her without knowing how to do that?"

We knew, of course, that the checkbook was an excuse. For Leonard, the opportunity to do one more good deed, the chance to wake up to one more beautiful day by the Hudson River, the prospect of another good discussion with Jane, with friends, with colleagues—he could not abandon all that.

So he had the next operation and, with the help of dozens of those detested medications, he is exercising and may be able to look forward to many more years of life. Of course, he still faces that question: What will I do with my life?

Lukas's Story _____

> What should I do with *my* renewal on life? After twelve years of living with cancer, after abdominal surgery in April 2003, at the age of sixty-eight, I am going strong, looking forward to the next opportunity. Well, what does that really mean? How many opportunities are there? Actually, I found quite a few only in the last year. I joined a community theater, where I've returned to doing acting—something I did all through adolescence and college. But now people say I'm good enough to do it professionally, so I'm taking acting classes, and I've begun auditioning. I'm practicing the piano an hour a day. I'm writing. And I'm still producing videos and television programs. There are lots of years and lots of projects I want to do. Cancer is *there*, but it's only a minor part of my conscious life.

_____

Quality of Life at the End of Life

So we come back to the basic question: how can you and those you love use the years you have left for real living, living with quality? Some things aren't in your control—the course of your disease, the workings of "the system," insurers' coverage policies, to name just a few. But much of the control over how you deal with a chronic or terminal illness *is* in your hands. And that's precisely where you want it! It's your life. It should be controlled as much as possible by you.

Last Acts Partnership offers a list of things that any of us can do to help make things happen and to increase our quality of life. You and your family should expect to get good care throughout any illness and at the end of life. You can improve the likelihood that you and your family will get the care you want if you:

- Discuss the care you want with your family, friends, physician and other health care professionals, and your spiritual adviser. Don't wait until you are seriously ill!

- Learn about your options for care. Make a list of questions to ask, to find out whether your doctor can provide the care you want near the end of life.
- Check with your local hospitals, nursing homes, and home health agencies about the special services (palliative care) they offer for dying patients and their families. Examples: Are there physicians, nurses, social workers and spiritual counselors trained in end-of-life care who can talk to you and your family about your concerns? Do they have experts who can manage pain and other physical discomforts? Do they offer bereavement services?
- Find out about local hospice services.
- Think about important decisions now. Prepare a living will and appoint someone to make decisions for you if you are not able.
- Look into community support groups and educational programs for seriously ill patients and their families (often offered by church groups, community centers, libraries, and other organizations).
- Get used to talking about the final years of your life. Don't shy away from it. Think about what you want those years to be and what you don't want them to be. In other words, think ahead, think bravely, think early.
- Share your thoughts with your family and health care team.
- Serve as a health care agent for someone else. The conversations become easier and easier the more you have.
- Do not wait to prepare yourself until you or someone you know and love is ill, or even diagnosed with a serious problem.
- Do not wait to prepare yourself until the point you can no longer make these decisions sensibly and with plenty of time to change your mind.
- Do not wait, because waiting will only give you fewer chances to think about the last years of your life; because waiting will not afford you the opportunity to choose an agent wisely; because waiting is what we all have done for too many years, for too many seasons.

The obstacles are being removed. Health care is moving in the direction of thinking about palliative care and hospice as the norm in the midst of trying to cure you and your disease. Forces are at work to make America a country where care and caring near the end of life are beginning to improve.

The rest is up to you.

You are at the heart of this revolution.

You are the reason why it is needed.

You are the reason it is happening.

You can make it better by taking control of your own life and helping those around you take control of theirs.

It's time to care about someone you love.

It's time to care about yourself.

Suggested Reading

There are hundreds of books that are meant to help deal with illness and dying. Some are intended for professionals, others for the general public. Some are filled with philosophy and spiritual advice, others are down-to-earth. Some deal with specific elements of illness—the physical or the emotional—others may approach a specific relationship or disease. While none of the following takes the same approach that we do, our feeling is that each is worth noting.

Address, Richard F. (*editor*) and the Commission on Jewish Family Concerns. *A Time to Prepare.* NY: Union of American Hebrew Congregations Press, 2002.

Anderson, Patricia. *All of Us: Americans Talk about the Meaning of Death.* NY: Dell, 1996.

Bernstein, Judith R. *When the Bough Breaks: Forever After the Death of a Son or Daughter.* Kansas City, MO: Andrews McMeel Publishing, 1998.

Byock, Ira. *Dying Well: The Prospect for Growth at the End of Life.* NY: Riverhead Books, 1997.

Callanan, Maggie, and Patricia Kelley. *Final Gifts: Understanding the Special Awareness, Needs, and Communications of the Dying.* NY: Bantam, 1997.

Dubler, Nancy Neveloff, and David Nimmons. *Ethics on Call: A Medical Enthusiast Shows How to Take Charge of Life-and-Death Choices in Today's Health Care System.* NY: Harmony Books, 1992.

Fins, Joseph, and Barbara Maltby. *Fidelity, Wisdom & Love: Patients and Proxies in Partnership.* (Call 860 828 2976 for copies of book and videotape.)

Furman, Joan, and David McNabb. *The Dying Time: Practical Wisdom for the Dying and Their Caregivers.* NY: Harmony/Bell Tower, 1997.

Gordon, Harvey L. *Questions & Answers about Jewish Tradition and the Issues of Assisted Death*. NY: Union of American Hebrew Congregations Press, 1999.

Grollman, Earl. *Talking about Death: A Dialogue between Parent and Child*. Boston: Beacon Press, 1970.

Grollman, Earl (*editor*). *Bereaved Children and Teens: A Support Guide for Parents and Professionals*. NY: Harmony/Bell Tower 1998; Boston: Beacon Press, 1995.

Hendin, Herbert. *Seduced by Death: Doctors, Patients, and The Dutch Cure*. NY: W.W. Norton, 1997.

Keizer, Bert. *Dancing with Mister D: Notes on Life and Death*. NY: Doubleday, 1996.

Kübler-Ross, Elisabeth. *On Death and Dying*. NY: Scribner, 1997.

Lamm, Maurice. *Jewish Way in Death and Mourning*. NY: Jonathan David Publishers, 1998.

Larkin, Marilyn. *When Someone You Love Has Alzheimer's: What You Must Know, What You Can Do, and What You Should Expect . . .* NY: Dell, A Lynn Sonberg Book, 1998.

Larue, Gerald. *Playing God: Deciding Your Life and Death*. Kingston, RI: Moyer Bell Ltd., 1996.

Levine, Stephen. *A Year to Live: How to Live This Year as If It Were Your Last*. NY: Harmony/Bell Tower, 1994.

Lukas, Christopher, and Henry Seiden. *Silent Grief: Living in the Wake of Suicide*. Northvale, NJ: Jason Aronson, 1997.

Lynn, Joanne (*editor*). *By No Extraordinary Means: The Choice to Forgo Life-Sustaining Food and Water*. IN: Indiana University Press, 1998.

McLeod, Beth Witrogen. *Caregiving: The Spiritual Journey of Love, Loss, and Renewal*. NY: John Wiley & Sons, 1999.

Nuland, Sherwin. *How We Die: Reflections on Life's Final Chapter*. NY: Vintage, 1995.

Quill, Timothy. *Death and Dignity: Making Choices and Taking Charge*. NY: W.W. Norton, 1994.

Quindlen, Anna. *One True Thing*. NY: Dell, 1995.

Radio and Television News Directors Foundation. *Covering the Issues of Death and Dying: A Journalist's Resource Guide*. Washington, D.C., 1998. (Published with support from Robert Wood Johnson Foundation.)

Ray, M. Catherine. *I'm Here to Help: A Guide for Caregivers, Hospice Workers, and Volunteers*. NY: Bantam, 1997.

Rinpoche, Sogyal, *The Tibetan Book of Living and Dying*. San Francisco: Harper, 1994.

Rollin, Betty. *Last Wish*. NY: PublicAffairs, 1998.

Rosenblum, Daniel. *A Time to Hear, a Time to Help: Listening to People with Cancer.* NY: The Free Press, 1993.

Spiro, Howard, Mary McCrea Curnen, and Lee Palmer Wandel (*editors*). *Facing Death: Where Culture, Religion, and Medicine Meet.* New Haven, CT: Yale University Press, 1992.

Tobin, Daniel R., with Karen Lindsey. *Peaceful Dying.* Cambridge, MA: Perseus Publishing, 1999.

Wilcock, Penelope. *Spiritual Care of Dying and Bereaved People.* Harrisburg, PA: Moorehouse Publishing, 1996.

Resources

What follows is a long list, but it is an extremely valuable one, because it tells you where to find help or advice or individuals who can address personally and with great specificity *your* particular need at any particular time. We've broken these resources down into categories you are likely to find useful. For that reason, some organizations appear more than once, when they are applicable to more than one category. Most of these organizations can be found on the Internet.

General Web Sites We Find Particularly Helpful

- www.lastactspartnership.org (free state-specific advance directives and instructions)
- www.LastChapters.org (stories about living with dying)
- www.PartnershipforCaring.org (specific information for individuals)

Advance Directives

Agency for Health Care Research and Quality—a research branch of the U.S. Department of Health and Human Services. The following will get you a wonderfully detailed analysis of how to improve conversation between physicians and patients about advance directives: www.ahcpr .gov/research/endliferia/endria.htm

Aging with Dignity
1-888-5-WISHES
www.agingwithdignity.org
provides the Five Wishes Living Will, legal in 33 states ($5 fee)

AARP
601 E St., NW
Washington, DC 20049
1-800-424-3410
www.aarp.org/endoflife
information on obtaining and completing advance directives

American Medical Association
515 N. State Street
Chicago, IL 60610
(312) 464-5000
www.ama-assn.org/public/booklets/ livgwill.htm
booklet on advance directives

Last Acts Partnership (formerly,
 Partnership for Caring: America's
 Voices for the Dying)
 1620 Eye St., NW, Suite 200
 Washington, DC 20006
 Hotline: 1-800-989-9455 (option 2)
 www.lastactspartnership.org
 provides free, state-specific living wills

U.S. Department of Health and Human
 Services
 www.hcfa.gov/pubforms/advdir.htm
 guidelines on advance directives

Gundersen Lutheran End-of-Life Care
 1836-1910 South Avenue
 La Crosse, WI 54601-5494
 (608) 782-7300 or 1-800-362-9567
 www.gundluth.org/eolprograms
 programs that help health care
  providers implement advance
  directives distribution in hospitals

Alzheimer's Disease

The Alzheimer Page
 www.biostat.wustl.edu/hyperlists/
  alzheimer
 a place to post and read personal
  stories about coping with caregiving to Alzheimer's patients

Alzheimer Web
 www.werple.mira.net.au/~dhs/ad.html
 provides basic information, research
  developments, links to international Alzheimer's resources, and a
  chat forum for caregivers

Alzheimer's Disease and Related
 Disorders Association
 919 N. Michigan Avenue, Suite 100
 Chicago, IL 60611
 1-800-272-3900
 provides general information on the
  disease and referrals to over 200
  local association chapters for
  specific services

Caregiving

www.Care-giver.com

Caring Road Interactive site
 www.caringroad.com
 offers support and information for
  caregivers, including chat rooms,
  links, and a disease directory

Empowering Care-givers
 www.care-givers.com
 a comprehensive site offering information, emotional and spiritual
  support through featured expert
  columns, articles on caregiving,
  journal exercises, a newsletter,
  forums, chats, healing circle, caregiver and caregiving spotlights,
  inspiration, humor and more

Family Care-giver Alliance
 690 Market Street, Suite 600
 San Francisco, CA 94104
 (415) 434-3388
 www.Care-giver.org
 provides resources, including information about specific diseases and
  related public policy news

Interfaith Volunteer Care-givers
 www.nfivc.org
 news and information about this
  national network of caregiving programs, with online forum for sharing personal stories

The National Alliance for Care-giving
 4720 Montgomery Lane, Suite 642
 Bethesda, MD 20814
 www.Care-giving.org
 provides information from pertinent
  studies, tips for caregivers, and a
  searchable resources directory

The National Family Care-givers
 Association
 10400 Connecticut Avenue, #500
 Kensington, MD 20895-3944

1-800-896-3650
www.nfcacares.org
offers practical information and
answers to frequently asked questions (FAQs), as well as "A Guide
to Improving Doctor/Care-giver
Communication"

National Organization For Empowering
Care-givers
425 West 23rd Street, Suite 9B
New York, New York 10011
(212) 807-1204
www.care-givers.com

Rosalynn Carter Institute for Human
Development
Georgia Southwestern State
University
800 Wheatley Street
Americus, GA 31709
(229) 928-1234
e-mail: haigler@rci. gsw.edu

Children

Bereaved Parents of the USA
P.O. Box 95
Park Forest, IL 60466
Fax (708) 748-9184
www.bereavedparentsusa.org
offers information and support to
parents and families who are struggling with the death of a child

The Candlelighters Childhood Cancer
Foundation
3910 Warner Street
Kensington, MD 20895
1-800-366-2223
www.candlelighters.org
offers support, advocacy and information to parents caring for children
with cancer

The National Organization for Rare
Disorders, Inc.
P.O. Box 8923
New Fairfield, CT 06812-8923

(203) 746-6518
www.rarediseases.org/index.html
provides information about rare
pediatric illnesses

The Compassionate Friends
P.O. Box 3696
Oak Brook IL 60522-3696
(877) 969-0010
www.compassionatefriends.org
provides grief support after the death
of a child

Pediatric Pain-Science Helping Children
IWK Grace Health Center, Dalhousie
University
Halifax, Nova Scotia
Canada
is.dal.ca/~pedpain/pedpain.html
offers resources, information and self-
help for parents

Project Joy and Hope for Texas
PO Box 5111
Pasadena, TX 77508
(713) 944-6JOY or toll free at
(866) JOYHOPE
www.joyandhope.org/contact.html
offers news and resource information
about end-of-life care and bereavement services for families with
children with life-limiting illness

Children's International Project on
Palliative/Hospice Services (ChIPPS)
National Hospice and Palliative Care
Organization
1700 Diagonal Road, Suite 300
Alexandria, VA 22314
(703) 837-1500
www.nhpco.org
offers information on the program to
enhance the science and practice of
pediatric hospice and palliative care

Children's Hospice International
2202 Mt. Vernon Ave, Suite 3C
Alexandria, VA 22301

1-800-24-CHILD or (703) 684-0330
www.chionline.org
offers information on children's
hospice care

Texas Children's Cancer Center
Texas Children's Hospital
6621 Fannin St.
Houston, TX 77030
www.childendoflifecare.org/home
.html
offers information and resources for
families and professionals on end-
of-life care for children; also offers
The End-of-Life Care for Children
handbook, which encompasses
most of the materials on the Web
site

Conversations before the Crisis

Aging with Dignity
The Five Wishes Project
1-888-5-WISHES
www.agingwithdignity.org
offers advance directive forms that can
be used by residents of 33 states

American Association of Retired Persons
601 E St., NW
Washington, DC 20049
1-800-424-3410
www.aarp.org/mmaturity/sept_oct00/
conversation.html
AARP's End-of-Life page offers
information on having end-of-life
conversations

Last Acts Partnership (formerly, Partnership for Caring: America's Voices for
the Dying)
PFC Publications—Publications
Office
1620 Eye St., NW, Suite 200
Washington, DC 20006
Hotline: 1-800-989-9455 (option 2)
www.lastactspartnership.org/

Talking/index.html
It's All About Talking page

The Midwest Bioethics Center
1021-1025 Jefferson Street
Kansas City, MO 64105
1-800-344-3829
www.midbio.org
makes available *Caring Conversations,*
(www.midbio.org/workbook.pdf),
a workbook to help start conversations, including advance health
care planning and advance directive forms

Culture & Diversity

ACCESS to End-of-Life Care: A
Community Initiative
P.O. Box 460478
San Francisco, CA 94146-0478
www.access2eolcare.org
formed in 1997 by a group of experienced hospice nurses, social workers, and administrators, this advocacy group provides education
about death, dying, and grieving

Assuring Cultural Competence in
Health Care
OMH Resource Center
P.O. Box 37337
Washington, DC 20013-7337
1-800-444-6472
http://www.omhrc.gov/clas/
the Health and Human Services
Office of Minority Health has published national standards on cultur-
ally and linguistically appropriate
services (CLAS) in health care,
available online

Growth House Inc.
www.growthhouse.org/
provides background and health
agency referral services with a
strong focus on diversity, including
a section on gay and lesbian issues

Tuskegee University National Center for
   Bioethics in Research & Health Care
   Tuskegee Institute
   1209 Chambliss Street
   Tuskegee, AL 36088
   (334)-724-4612
   www.tubioethics.org
   devoted to engaging the sciences,
      humanities, law, and religious
      faiths in exploring moral issues
      involving research and medical
      treatment of African Americans
      and other underserved people, the
      Center provides leadership in
      cultural diversity and death and
      dying

Grief & Loss

AARP Grief and Loss Programs
   601 E Street, NW
   Washington, DC 20049
   (202) 434-2260
   www.aarp.org/griefandloss
   offers a variety of programs in which
      volunteers reach out to widows

The Center for Grieving Children
   49 York Street
   P.O. Box 1438
   Portland, ME 04104
   (207) 775-5216
   www.cgcmaine.org
   provides educational and support
      materials to grieving children,
      teens, their families, schools, and
      other community agencies who
      support them

The Compassionate Friends
   P.O. Box 3696
   Oakbrook, IL 60522
   (877) 969-0010
   www.compassionatefriends.org
   for parents who have lost
      a child

ElderHope, LLC
   P.O. Box 940822
   Plano, TX 75094-0822
   (972) 768-8553
   www.elderhope.com
   offers online support, forums,
      seminars, classes, and bereavement
      materials

Hospice Foundation of America
   2001 S Street, NW, Suite 300
   Washington, DC 20009
   (202) 638-5419 or 1-800-854-3402
   www.hospicefoundation.org
   offers information to professionals
      and families about caregiving, ter-
      minal illness, loss, and bereave-
      ment; their monthly newsletter,
      Journeys, is a valuable tool for any
      and all forms of loss

Parents Without Partners
   1650 S. Dixie Highway, Suite 510
   Boca Raton, FL 33432
   (561) 391-8833
   www.parentswithoutpartners.org
   offers support, information and
      resources for single parents

HIV/AIDS

AIDS Hotline
   1-800-342-AIDS (2437)
   Operated by the Centers for Disease
      Control and Prevention; provides
      general information about AIDS
      and HIV, as well as referrals to
      HIV testing facilities, medical serv-
      ices, counseling, and support
      groups. There is someone available
      to answer calls 24 hours a day and
      they maintain a national database
      of AIDS resources.

AIDS Pastoral Care Network
   4753 North Broadway, Suite 800
   Chicago, IL 60640

(312) 334-5333
(312) 334-3293 [fax]

HIVInSite
http://hivinsite.ucsf.edu
the University of California San
    Francisco offers comprehensive
    information on issues surrounding
    HIV/AIDS

Hospice

American Academy of Hospice and
    Palliative Medicine
4700 W. Lake Ave.
Glenview, IL 60025-1485
(847) 375-4712
www.aahpm.org
includes a selection of links to general
    hospice informational sites

American Hospice Foundation
2120 L Street, NW, Suite 200
Washington, DC 20037
(202) 223-0204
www.americanhospice.org
includes a collection of articles with
    practical information for the dying
    or the grieving; offers *Grief at
    School Training Guide & Video* to
    help teachers respond to grieving
    children and on-site training
    workshops

Hospice Foundation of America
2001 S Street, NW, Suite 300
Washington, DC 20009
(202) 638-5419 or 1-800-854-3402
www.hospicefoundation.org
the site provides guidelines for
    choosing hospice, tips for dealing
    with grief and other consumer
    resources, such as a collection of
    hospice readings and Web links.
    Call the foundation to find a hos-
    pice near you.

The Hospice and Palliative Nurses
    Association
Penn Center West One, Suite 229
Pittsburgh, PA 15276
(412) 787-9301
www.hpna.org
check on background and credentials
    for hospice nurses

Hospicelink (Hospice Education
    Institute)
1-800-331-1620
provides general information on
    hospice care and referrals to hos-
    pices across the country

HospiceWeb
www.hospiceweb.com
offers a message board, a list of
    answers to frequently asked ques-
    tions (FAQs) about hospice, and
    links to numerous hospice-related
    sites throughout the world

National Association for Home Care
www.nahc.org
extensive listings of publications and
    videos for professional and general
    audiences, plus a directory of over
    19,500 home care and hospice
    agencies

National Hospice Foundation
1700 Diagonal Rd., Suite 300
Alexandria, VA 22314
(703) 516-4928
www.hospiceinfo.org
informs the public about the quality
    end-of-life care that hospice pro-
    vides, including information on
    choosing a hospice and communi-
    cating your end-of-life wishes

National Hospice and Palliative Care
    Organization
1700 Diagonal Road, Suite 300
Alexandria, VA 22314
(703) 837-1500

www.nhpco.org
offers a hospice database and provides statistical and educational material about hospice care, or call the toll-free HelpLine at (800) 658-8898 to find a hospice near you

Last Rites

The American Association for Death Education and Counseling
342 North Main Street
West Hartford, CT 06117-2507
(860) 586-7503
www.adec.org
a professional organization dedicated to promoting excellence in death education, bereavement counseling, and care of the dying

Beliefnet
www.beliefnet.com
billing itself as the "source for spirituality, religion and morality," Beliefnet is an online community that offers comprehensive information on death, grief, bereavement and funerals; especially worthy are this site's comparative religion features

The Funeral Consumers Alliance
P.O. Box 10
Hinesburg, VT
(802) 482-3437
www.funerals.org
provides information for consumers about funeral ethics, affordability, and legal issues

"Funerals: A Consumer's Guide"
1-877-FTC-HELP
www.ftc.gov/bcp/conline/pubs/services/funeral.htm
published by the Federal Trade Commission

The National Funeral Directors Association
13625 Bishop's Drive
Brookfield, WI 53005
1-800-228-6332
www.nfda.org
offers useful consumer guidelines, demographic information, and helpful links to other national and international organizations

Nursing Homes & Long Term Care

Medicare's Website
www.medicare.gov/Nursing/Overview.asp
offers the Nursing Home Compare database, with information about every Medicare/Medicaid certified nursing home in the country, organized by state, county, and city

National Association for Home Care/Hospice Association of America
228 Seventh St., SE
Washington, DC 20003
Contact: Karen Woods, HAA
Executive Director (202) 546-4759
(202) 547-7424
(202)547-3540 [fax]
www.nahc.org/home.html
since 1982, NAHC has remained committed to serving the home care and hospice industry, which provides services to the sick, the disabled, and the terminally ill in the comfort of their homes

Your Guide to Choosing a Nursing Home
7500 Security Boulevard
Baltimore, MD 21244
1-800-633-4227
www.medicare.gov/Publications/Pubs/pdf/nhguide.pdf

a booklet available from the Health Care Financing Administration of the U.S. Department of Health and Human Services

Palliative Care and Pain Management

American Academy of Hospice and Palliative Medicine
4700 W. Lake Ave.
Glenview, IL 60025-1485
(847) 375-4712
www.aahpm.org
find board-certified hospice and palliative care physicians

American Academy of Pain Management
13947 Mono Way #A
Sonora, CA 95370
Contact: Richard S. Weiner, Ph.D., Executive Director
(209) 533-9744
(209)545-2920 [fax]

American Academy of Pain Medicine
4700 West Lake Av.
Glenview, IL 60025-1485
(847) 375-4731
(847) 375-4777 [fax]

American Board of Hospice and Palliative Medicine
9200 Daleview Court
Silver Spring, MD 20901
(301) 439-8001
www.abhpm.org
provides information on palliative care and a directory of ABHPM-certified physicians

American Chronic Pain Association
P.O. Box 850
Rocklin, CA 95677-0850
Contact: Penny Cowan
(916) 632-0922
(916) 632-3208 [fax]

American Medical Association, Institute for Ethics
515 N. State St.
Chicago, IL 60610
(312) 464-4979
www.ama-assn.org
EPEC (Education for Physicians on End of Life Care Project) offers information on end-of-life care education for professionals

The American Pain Foundation
201 N. Charles Street, Suite 710
Baltimore, MD 21201-4111
www.painfoundation.org
provides a survey to screen yourself for depression and access to on-line support

American Pain Society
5700 Old Orchard Road, First Floor
Skokie, IL 60077
(847) 375-4715
association of pain physicians; provides referrals to pain facilities, physicians, and support groups

American Society of Pain Management Nurses
1550 South Coast Highway, Suite 201
Laguna Beach, CA 92651
Contact: Kim Hererra, Executive Director
(888) 342-7755

The Center for Advanced Illness Coordinated Care, in collaboration with the Veterans Administration Healthcare Network of Upstate New York at Albany
113 Holland Avenue (111t)
Albany, NY 12208
(518) 626-6088
www.coordinatedcare.net

find guidance on coping with the complexities of serious illness through the "Walking the Advanced Illness Road" section

City of Hope National Medical Center
Mayday Pain Resource Center
1500 E. Duarte Rd.
Duarte, CA 91010
Contact: Betty Ferrell
(626) 359-8111
www.cityofhope.org/medinfo/mayday.htm
a clearinghouse to disseminate information and resources for improving the quality of pain management

Department of Symptom Control and Palliative Care
M. D. Anderson Cancer Center
1515 Holcombe, Box 08
Houston, TX 77030
(713) 792-6085
www.mdanderson.org/departments/palliative/
provides information and resources about symptom control and palliative care

Growth House
San Francisco, CA
(415) 255-9045
www.growthhouse.org
excellent source for books and other publications regarding end-of-life care

Palliative Care Corner
13947 Silven Ave NE
Bainbridge Island, WA 98110
(206) 855-8026
www.painconsult.com
offers resources for patients and providers

Palliative Care Initiative
Mount Sinai School of Medicine
Mount Sinai Medical Center
1 Gustave L. Levy Place
New York, NY 10029

Palliative Care Overview
www.medbroadcast.com/health_topics/death_dying/
provides an overview of palliative care and pain treatment

Society for Pain Practice Management
11111 Nall, # 202
Leawood, KS 66211
Contact: David Waldman, JD, Executive Director
(913) 491-6451
(913) 491-6453 [fax]

Spirituality & Faith

American Association of Pastoral Counselors
9504-A Lee Highway
Fairfax, VA 22031
(703) 385-6967
www.aapc.org
provides information about pastoral counseling, resources and a searchable directory of pastoral counselors

Compassion Sabbath
1021-1025 Jefferson St.
Kansas City, MO 64105
(816) 221-1100
www.midbio.org/cs/index.htm
an interfaith initiative to help clergy and congregations minister to seriously ill and dying people

Ethical Wills
www.ethicalwill.com
offers a way to leave your legacy by writing down your values and beliefs

Gilda's Club Worldwide
5 Madison Ave., Suite 609
New York, NY 10016
(212) 686-9898
www.gildasclub.org
offers emotional and social support to those living with cancer and their families

Supportive Care of the Dying: A Coalition for Compassionate Care
c/o Providence Health System
4805 NE Glisan St., 2E07
Portland, OR 97213
Contact: Sylvia McSkimming, Executive Director
(503) 215-5053
(503) 215-5054 [fax]
e-mail: Sylvia_McSkimming@ phsor.org
an initiative of 11 Catholic health systems and the Catholic Health Association to develop a new model of care for the dying

The George Washington Institute for Spirituality and Health
2131 K Street, NW, Suite 510
Washington, DC 20037-1898
202-496-6406
202-496-6413 [fax]
hcscmp@gwumc.edu

Violence and Unexpected Death (Including Suicide)

American Association of Suicidology
4201 Connecticut Ave., NW
Suite 408
Washington, DC 20008
(202) 237-2280
www.suicidology.org
devoted to understanding and preventing suicide, this organization also has a strong support system for those left behind after the suicide of a relative or friend

American Foundation for Suicide Prevention
120 Wall Street, 22nd Floor
New York, New York 10005
(888) 333-AFSP/(212) 363-3500
(212) 363-6237 [fax]
email: inquiry@afsp.org

Bereaved Parents of the USA
P.O. Box 95
Park Forest, IL 60466
fax (708) 748-9184
www.bereavedparentsusa.org
offers information and support to parents and families who are struggling with the death of a child

The Compassionate Friends
P.O. Box 3696
Oak Brook IL 60522-3696
(877) 969-0010
www.compassionatefriends.org
provides grief support after the death of a child

Mothers Against Drunk Driving (MADD)
(214) 744-6233/1-800-GET-MADD
www.madd.org
an organization working to stop drunk driving, support the victims of this violent crime, and prevent underage drinking

National Organization for Victim Assistance
1730 Park Road NW
Washington, DC 20010
(202) 232-6682 or
1-800-TRY-NOVA
www.try-nova.org
provides information about victim's rights, assistance and services

Parents of Murdered Children
National POMC
100 East Eighth Street, Suite B-41

Cincinnati, OH 45202
(513) 721-5683 or
1-888-818-POMC
www.pomc.com
provides resources, support, and
advocacy information to parents of
murdered children

General & Miscellaneous

Alliance for Aging Research
2021 K St., NW, Suite 305
Washington, DC 20006
Contact: Daniel Perry, Executive
Director
(202) 293-2856
www.agingresearch.org
this group's study, *Seven Deadly
Myths: Uncovering the Facts About
the High Cost of the Last Year of
Life,* explores—and explodes—
some common assumptions about
the costs of end-of-life care, based
on a review of Medicare data and
the medical literature

ALS Association
2101 Ventura Boulevard, Suite 321
Woodland, CA 91364
1-800-782-4747
provides information and educational
materials about ALS (Lou Gehrig's
Disease); will provide referrals to
physicians, support groups, and
drug trials

Americans for Better Care of the Dying
4200 Wisconsin Avenue, NW,
4th Floor
(202) 895-2660
(202) 966-5410 [fax]
e-mail: info@abcd-caring.org
www.abcd-caring.org
track changes in public policy, as well
as reforms in pain management
and support for family caregivers

Cancer Care, Inc.
1180 Avenue of the Americas
New York, NY 10036
1-800-813-HOPE (4673)
(212) 302-2400
cancercare@aol.com
www.cancercare.org
provides support groups, educational
programs, and workshops for cancer patients and their families.
They operate a national referral
service, and counselors on staff
provide assistance to callers. Cancer
Care also publishes *Helping Hand,*
a useful resource guide for cancer
patients and others.

Cancer Information Service
1-800-4-CANCER (422-6237)
has 19 offices across the country.
Answers any question related to
cancer and cancer treatment;
provides referrals to hospice,
home care, and support groups

Center to Advance Palliative Care
Mount Sinai Hospital
1 Gustave L. Levy Place, Box 1070
New York, NY 10029-6547
www.capcmssm.org
search the latest resources in palliative
care available to hospitals and
health care systems

Center for Palliative Care Studies
4200 Wisconsin Avenue, N.W.,
4th floor
Washington, DC 20016
(202) 895-2625
(202) 966-5410 [fax]
info@medicaring.org
www.medicaring.org
www.gwu.edu/~cicd
CPCS offers expert support to
hospitals, nursing homes, health
systems, hospices, and other

organizations that serve individuals nearing the end of life

Committee on Care at the End of Life
Report: *Approaching Death: Improving Care at the End of Life*
2101 Constitution Av., NW
Washington, DC 20418
Media Contact: Dan Quinn
E-mail: news@nas.edu
(202) 334-2138
Approaching Death: Improving Care at the End of Life is the result of information gathered between January 1996 and January 1997 by a committee of end-of-life experts including ethicists, physicians, and health policy specialists. The study offers data, analysis, case studies, and extensive reading lists and resources. The public can receive a copy of the report from:
The American Academy of Hospice and Palliative Medicine
11250 Roger Bacon Drive, Suite 8
Reston, VA 20190
(703) 787-7718, (703) 435-3390

Growth House
(415) 255-9045
www.growthhouse.org
excellent source for books and other publications regarding end-of-life care

Last Acts Partnership (formerly Partnership for Caring: America's Voices for the Dying)
1620 Eye St., NW, Suite 200
Washington, DC 20006
Hotline: 1-800-989-9455 (option 2)
www. lastactspartnership.org
provides free, state-specific living wills

National Hospice and Palliative Care Organization
1700 Diagonal Road, Suite 300
Alexandria, VA 22314
(703) 837-1500
www.NHPCO.org
provides a search for hospice and palliative care, as well as statistics, resources, and information

National Self-Help Clearinghouse
25 W. 43rd Street, Room 620
New York, NY 10036
(212) 642-2944
www.selfhelpweb.org
part of a countrywide affiliation of clearinghouses; provides referrals to self-help organizations; mutual-support groups; and other national, state, local and community resources

Promoting Excellence in End-of-Life Care
The University of Montana
1000 East Beckwith Avenue
Missoula, MT 59812
(406) 243-6601
www.endoflifecare.org
researches innovative programs that have received grants and technical support to change the face of dying in America

Visiting Nurse Association of America
11 Beacon Street, Suite 910
Boston, MA 02108
(888) 866-8773 or (617) 523-4042
(617) 227-4843 [fax]
provides referrals to visiting nurse agencies nationwide and supports visiting nurse agencies in their commitment to provide the most effective, innovative, and personalized community-based care

Acknowledgments

We would like to acknowledge all the people who have helped us with this book, but that's not possible: there are too many. There are all the hospice workers and palliative care specialists who work endlessly to comfort the seriously ill and dying; the lawyers who helped Choice in Dying devise living wills; the ethicists who work day in, day out to figure out the rights and wrongs of end-of-life care; and the patients who have given freely of their emotional and physical time.

We can thank our spouses, Marshall and Susan, for understanding why we were absent or at the computer for so long, and for believing in our task. We can and do thank colleagues and friends at Last Acts Partnership; our editor, Lisa Considine, for pushing harder than we wanted to be pushed; and our agent, Jennifer Unter, who didn't give up on offering this book to publishers.

Index